Gilmore girls™

Gilmore girls™

THE OFFICIAL COOKBOOK

Recipes by **ELENA P. CRAIG**

Text by **KRISTEN MULROONEY**

TITAN BOOKS

LONDON

CONTENTS

7   *Introduction*

13   **CHAPTER 1**
Luke's Diner

15   Coffee in an IV:
Tips on Brewing Strong Coffee

16   Hot Fudge Sundae With
Grapefruit on the Side

17   Luke's Special Omelet

19   Fluffy Buttermilk Pancakes

20   Classic Luke's Diner Cheeseburger

23   Luke's Health-Conscious
Turkey Burger

25   Santa Burger

26   Chili Cheese Fries

27   Caesar's Salad

28   Delicious Donuts

30   Chicken Noodle Soup

31   Side of Mashed Potatoes

33   Danish Day Danishes

35   Perfect Peach Pie

36   Caesar's Chilaquiles!

39   **CHAPTER 2**
*The Independence Inn,
The Dragonfly Inn, &
Sookie St. James's Creations*

41   Roquefort Puffs

42   Jackson's Blueberry Shortcake

44   Sookie's Magic Risotto

47   Sookie's Wedding Cake & Cupcakes

50   Deep-Fried Turkey Leg

51   Medieval Feast Plum Pudding

53   Sookie's Critically Acclaimed Zucchini Soup

54   Sookie's Survival Margaritas

56   Jalapeño-Chipotle Mac & Cheese

57   Lobster Bisque

59   Lorelai's Graduation Cake

63   Ciabatta Bun Caprese Sandwiches

64   Sookie's Roasted Acorn Squash Soup

67   Norman Mailer's Legendary Iced Tea

69   Broccoli Tarts

70   Handkerchief Pasta With Brown Butter Sauce

STARS HOLLOW
FOUNDED · 1779 ·

73 CHAPTER 3

A Stars Hollow Potluck

75 Mrs. Kim's Eggless Egg Salad Sandwiches

76 Mrs. Kim's Everything-Free Muffin Drops & Tea

77 Mrs. Kim's Extra Chunky Multigrain Pudding

78 Lane's Wedding Dumplings

82 Pasta 3 Ways for Rory & Dean's Three-Month Anniversary

86 Cashew Chicken

89 Vegetable Chow Mein

90 Red Velvet Cake

91 Ye Olde Butter Brickle Crunch Ice Cream

92 Lorelai's Giant Birthday Pizza

94 Steak & Six Baked Potatoes for Four People

97 Beef Noodle Salad

98 Shrimp from Al's Pancake World

100 Founder's Day Punch

103 CHAPTER 4

Lorelai & Rory's House

105 Movie Night Snack Board

106 Homemade Peanut Butter Sandwich Cookies

109 Homemade Edible Cookie Dough

110 Rory's Pretzels from Around the World

112 Lime Fantasy Supreme With Two Spoons

115 Dessert Sushi

116 Cream Puffs for Hands

118 Frozen Pizza With Tater Tots

119 Complete Salad in a Bag

121 Wallowing Board

122 Nachos & a Slushie

123 Apple & Cherry Turnovers

125 Homemade Toaster Pastries

129 CHAPTER 5

Beyond Stars Hollow

131 Friday Night Dinner With Emily & Richard

131   Pot Roast, Potatoes, and Rolls

134   Chocolate Cake & Coffee

138 Dark Chocolate Pudding

139 Gin Martini No Onion

141 The Rory Drink

142 Emily's Tailgate Bloody Marys

144 Mashed Bananas on Toast

145 Logan's Surprise Gazpacho

146 Lobster Pot Pie

148 Trix's Spiced Nuts

149 Johnny Machette's Pasta Casserole

151 Salmon Puffs

152 Rosa's Lamb Sandwich

153 Rosa's Strudel

154 Funky Monkey Drink

156 Hector's Tacos

157 Spring Break Fruit Plate

159 Christmas Apple Tarts

161 *Conclusion: Bon Voyage*

162 *About the Authors*

165 *Dietary Considerations*

166 *Glossary*

169 *Measurement Conversions*

170 *Notes*

172 *Index*

Introduction

There's never been a town quite like Stars Hollow. The tiny hamlet in Connecticut, home to Lorelai and Rory Gilmore and their motley community of unique neighbors, is whimsical in a way most of us can only dream about. Who wouldn't want to be there when the first snow falls during the winter festival; or to stroll through the pumpkin patch in March (the pumpkins came in late that year); or to walk down the streets on a fall evening, breathing the cool autumn air with fairy lights twinkling all around you?

And it's not just the Taylor Doose-approved ambience that makes Stars Hollow so cozy. The close-knit neighborhood that welcomed a young Lorelai and baby Rory is the core of its charm. In Stars Hollow, doors are always open, and a neighbor is always willing to lend an ear, a hand, or a shoulder to cry on. After all, this is a community whose residents devoted town meeting time to organizing sleeping arrangements for Kirk.

Community and togetherness are such a huge theme in the show, and that theme is interwoven with a strong thread: FOOD. Food is unquestionably a major part of the Gilmore Girls universe, and it's not just there to make you hungry while you binge watch. In a world filled with rapid, chaotic chatter, even the food speaks. Mashed banana on toast says, "I care." A gin martini with an onion says, "I don't care." Cookie dough says, "I'm sad." Or, "I'm happy." Or, "I'm hungry." Or, "I'm not even hungry, but, boy, I bet that cookie dough tastes good!" Cookie dough says a lot of things actually. It's one of the more outspoken foods.

The sections in this book take us on a journey through the Gilmore Girls' culinary universe. You'll find some of the best recipes from Luke's Diner, Sookie's kitchen, Lorelai and Rory's house, and locations all around Stars Hollow and beyond. There's something for every palate: healthy, everything-free recipes courtesy of Mrs. Kim and tasty treats like donuts, toaster pastries, and dessert sushi for those with a sweet tooth and a disavowed sugar addiction. You'll find snacks for movie nights with friends and snacks for comfort after a breakup with the sweet boy from town or the bad boy from out of town.

So read up, eat up, and sometimes reheat up (those frozen tater tots aren't going to pop themselves in the oven) and enjoy the best recipes from some of our favorite episodes. Cook for your friends, family, and everyone in between who makes up your community, and let the food speak for you in those moments when you can't find the words—however unlikely those moments may be.

The PEOPLE of STARS HOLLOW

Stars Hollow is brought to life by the smorgasbord of people who live in it. Here are some of the notable neighbors and what they bring to the table.

LORELAI

Friend. Businesswoman. Coffee addict. Lorelai Gilmore wears many hats, but the one she wears most seriously is mother. Bona fide cool mom Lorelai made her way to Stars Hollow when Rory was a baby, and her effervescence cemented their spot in the community.

RORY

Smart and bookish Rory is the darling of Stars Hollow, even when she spreads her wings and ditches the public high school for the elite Chilton. The townspeople watched her grow up and are now super invested in every aspect of her life, from following her romantic scandals to making her the Ice Cream Queen.

LUKE

The owner of Stars Hollow's beloved diner is a reluctant pillar of the community. His love life is often the center of town gossip, much to his disdain, but he's still always there with a burger or a cup of coffee. Luke has a brooding nephew, Jess, and one surprise daughter, April.

DEAN

Dean is a good, if not overbearing, first boyfriend to Rory. And after they break up, he's a good, if not overbearing, friend to her. And then after he marries someone else, he's still very good to Rory—maybe a little *too* good (and, yes, slightly overbearing).

JESS

Nobody fits into Stars Hollow less than Jess Mariano. Luke's troubled, rebellious nephew manages to even get himself on Lorelai's bad side, and his reticent nature ends up breaking Rory's heart. In the end, it seems his time in Stars Hollow did him some good.

SOOKIE

Sookie's bubbly personality makes her a wonderful, supportive friend, but she isn't afraid to set anyone straight either, whether it's showing Lorelai her disapproval of Christopher or refusing Jackson's squash. Stars Hollow's resident chef is often found taking control of any kitchen she walks into.

JACKSON

As produce supplier for the Independence Inn, Jackson spent so much time in the kitchen trying to convince Sookie to buy his vegetables that he ended up marrying her. Aside from wanting Sookie to have four babies in four years, Jackson is one of the more grounded members of Stars Hollow and even briefly held the position of town selectman.

CHRISTOPHER

Rory's father was reluctant to grow up and settle down with Lorelai and Rory, but Christopher does eventually buy a Volvo, so that's progress. A perpetual wrench in Lorelai's life, he lives in Stars Hollow only briefly.

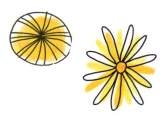

GILMORE *Romance* TREE

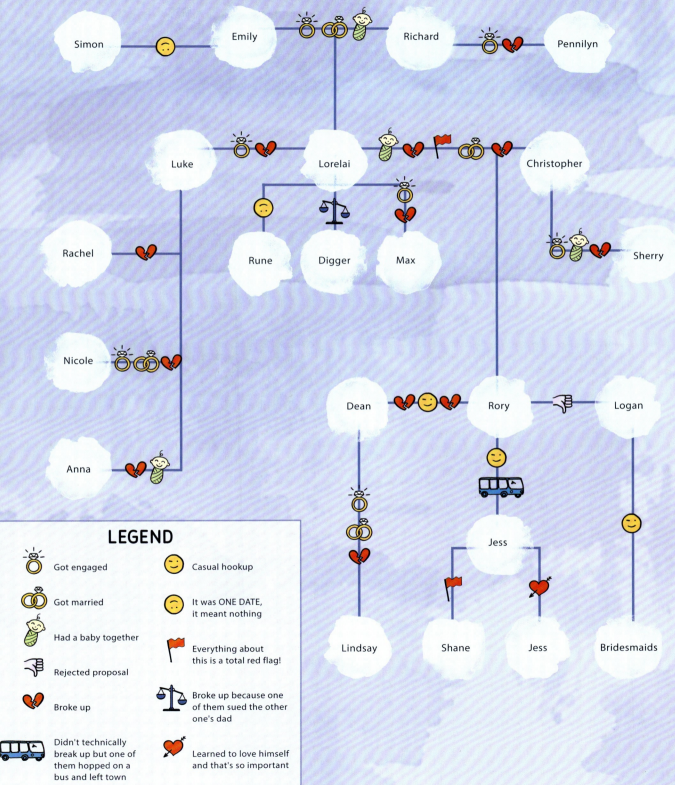

MICHEL

The acerbic concierge of the Independence Inn and Dragonfly Inn isn't exactly nice. Or polite. And, he rarely says anything that's not dripping in what the French call le sarcasme. Michel was devastated by the death of his Chow Chow Chin-Chin.

LANE

The best drummer in Stars Hollow has to do all of her drumming very quietly to keep it a secret from her conservative mother. Lane is full of energy and ideas, and she once had extremely purple hair for a full thirty minutes.

ZACK

Zack, the lead singer and guitarist of Hep Alien turned questionable boyfriend turned doting husband and father, can be a little slow on the uptake, but he's a good guy. Zack is embarrassed to admit he likes bluegrass music.

CAESAR

The chef at Luke's Diner is a real go-getter. Caesar isn't afraid to share some of his best recipes with Luke to expand the diner's menu, including Caesar's salad, cold bananas, and the ever-popular chilaquiles.

LULU

Everyone loves sweet elementary school teacher Lulu, and Lulu sure loves the Gleason boys. Once Kirk's brother's girlfriend, Lulu ends up falling for . . . Kirk? Her neighbors in Stars Hollow have a lot of questions, but, hey, there's a lid for every pot.

LIZ *and* TJ

Jess's mother Liz spent most of her adult life freewheeling. When she finds her soulmate in TJ, she finally settles down in Stars Hollow near her big brother Luke—but even the matured version of these wild lovers of everything renaissance is still pretty offbeat.

MAX

Rory's English teacher and Lorelai's ex-fiancé is a nice guy, but he never quite fit into the Gilmores' Stars Hollow life. He once took several minutes to decide what he wanted for breakfast at Luke's Diner. Unacceptable!

KIRK

A jack-of-all-trades and master of absolutely nothing, Kirk is the owner of a cat named Kirk, director of A Film by Kirk, and has held no less than sixty-two jobs in Stars Hollow. He does not live in his mother's basement bomb shelter (anymore).

TAYLOR

As the town selectman and owner of both Doose's Market and Taylor's Olde Fashioned Soda Shoppe, Taylor Doose is arguably the most powerful man in town. He's a stickler for statutes and loves pushing everyone's buttons to get his own way.

MISS PATTY

Patty is a former singer and dancer and the current owner of the dance studio in Stars Hollow. She always has the scoop on what's going on around town. Married four different times to three different husbands, Miss Patty's favorite snack is a handsome young man.

BABETTE

Lorelai and Rory's next-door neighbor loves her husband Morey and her cats: new kitten Apricot and the late Cinnamon. She's second only to Miss Patty when it comes to being on top of the town gossip. Babette is a sweet soul who was once thrown from a moving car.

MOREY

Babette's husband tends to blend into the background, despite being somewhere between six and ten feet tall. Morey is super chill and happy to do whatever Babette tells him. He's often found wearing sunglasses inside and playing the piano.

GYPSY

Stars Hollow's best mechanic is always ready with a wisecrack. She's never afraid to put Taylor in his place with a wry comeback, but her involvement in the community shows a soft spot for Stars Hollow and her neighbors.

ANDREW

The owner of Stars Hollow's Books uses his free time to participate in the town's Revolutionary "War" "reenactment." Andrew is unlucky in love and, quite frankly, kind of a bummer.

MRS. KIM

Mrs. Kim is Lane's mother and the owner of Kim's Antiques, which she runs out of her jam-packed home. She's highly suspicious of boys, rock music, Lorelai Gilmore, and many American customs.

The TROUBADOUR

Elected Stars Hollow's official troubadour at a town meeting, he is often seen troubadouring around the town square.

Luke's Diner

There's a reason *Gilmore Girls* begins and ends at Luke's Diner, and it's not just because it serves the world's best coffee. The diner, set in the center of Stars Hollow in the William's Hardware building, is Lorelai and Rory's home away from home. It's where the people of Stars Hollow go to sit and break bread and chat with their neighbors (not on the phone though—no cell phones allowed!).

Although the help is sometimes questionable (looking at you, Froggy), the atmospheric charm is more than enough to keep patrons coming back for more: the mismatched mugs, the leftover tools and hardware lining the shop, and, when Taylor can bully Luke into them, fairy lights and holiday decorations.

Come for the coffee, stay for the coffee, and maybe have a meal in between. Luke's door is always open; unless it's closed, in which case . . . go away.

COFFEE IN AN IV
Tips on Brewing Strong Coffee

There's a reason those Gilmore Girls have so much pep: they're fully caffeinated at every hour of the day, from the first swill of wake-up coffee in the morning to that last sip of bedtime coffee at night. Here are some tips for brewing the perfect coffee, whether you prefer double cafe, triple cafe, or the whole cow.

The perfect cup of coffee starts with the right grind. For flat-bottom filters, the grind should be medium grain, like a coarse salt. Cone-shaped filters need a finer grind, closer to the texture of sugar. Use one mounded scoop of ground coffee beans (or approximately 2 tablespoons) for every 6 ounces of water being brewed, plus an extra scoop for the pot! Lorelai likes her coffee strong, and that extra scoop helps kick it up a notch. If you don't like the taste of your tap water, then consider using cool filtered water to make your coffee.

Want to add a little something special? Before brewing, sprinkle the grounds with ¼ teaspoon of a spice, such as cinnamon or nutmeg, to add some warmth and depth to your brew.

Having a variety of add-ins for your coffee is a must! Lorelai and Rory drink their coffee in almost every way imaginable, so have all or at least some of these things on hand:

- Milk
- Half-and-half
- Vanilla paste
- Caramel and/or chocolate syrup
- Turbinado sugar
- Whipped cream

"This is a jumbo coffee morning. I need coffee in an IV."

LORELAI

HOT FUDGE SUNDAE
With Grapefruit
on the Side

In another attempt to get some nutrients into the Gilmores, Luke tries covertly serving half a grapefruit alongside Rory's hot fudge sundae. Grapefruit might sound like an unconventional side to a treasured dairy-based dessert, but the citrus and the rich chocolate are as compatible as Fred and Ginger, or Butch Cassidy and the Sundance Kid, or, Edith and Little Edie! Besides, grapefruit prevents scurvy. You can caramelize the grapefruit to sweeten it up and make your own hot fudge with this sweet and easy recipe.

YIELD: 4 servings

1 cup cream, divided
1 cup milk chocolate chips
1 cup semi-sweet chocolate chips
¼ cup turbinado sugar
1 ruby red grapefruit halved, then quartered, then cut into eight wedges
Vanilla ice cream
Whipped cream, optional

Pour ½ cup of cream, each, into two microwave-safe bowls. Bring the cream to scalding by separately microwaving each bowl for 1 to 1½ minutes. Pour the milk chocolate chips into one bowl of cream and the semi-sweet chocolate chips into the other and let stand without stirring for 5 minutes. Stir thoroughly to combine. Set aside until serving.

Line a rimmed baking sheet with a silicone baking mat or aluminum foil and turn on the oven's broiler.

Pour the turbinado sugar onto a shallow plate. Dip the sides of each grapefruit wedge into the sugar and coat both sides. Place on the baking sheet, rind side down.

Broil 2 to 3 minutes until the sugar has liquefied and the grapefruit is just beginning to brown. Remove from the oven and allow to cool.

To assemble, place 1 scoop of ice cream into each of four sundae glasses or bowls and drizzle with some of each chocolate sauce. Top with a second scoop of ice cream and repeat with the chocolate sauces. If using, top with whipped cream. Nestle two slices of grapefruit on top of each sundae and serve immediately.

LUKE: *"Here we go: boysenberry pie with ice cream, hot fudge sundae, half a grapefruit."*

RORY: *"I don't want a grapefruit."*

LUKE: *"It's good for you."*

RORY: *"Kinda my point."*

LUKE'S
Special Omelet

Luke throws Stars Hollow a curveball when he changes his special from the four-slice French toast that had been on the Specials menu sign since Rory was born to his Special Omelet. This breakfast special consists of three eggs with bits of bacon, diced tomatoes, Swiss cheese, and a dash of oregano. To Luke's surprise, this breakfast is a Lorelai favorite, as long as he omits the bacon. And the tomatoes. And the oregano. And subs the Swiss cheese for Jack.

YIELD: 1 omelet

3 eggs

¼ teaspoon of salt

Fresh ground pepper to taste

2 tablespoons unsalted butter, divided

¼ cup grated Swiss cheese

¼ Roma tomato, cored and finely diced

2 strips of bacon, cooked crisp and crumbled

1 teaspoon finely minced fresh oregano

In a medium bowl combine the eggs and salt (and pepper to taste). Whisk vigorously until the mixture is homogeneous without any streaks of egg white or yolk. The mixture should be slightly frothy.

Heat an 8-inch non-stick skillet or omelet pan over medium heat for 1 to 1½ minutes and then add 1 tablespoon butter.

Just as the butter begins to foam, add the egg mixture. Immediately start agitating the egg by stirring with a wooden spoon or chopsticks while shaking the pan with the other hand.

As soon as there is no liquid egg, turn the heat down to low and shake the pan to settle the eggs. Use a thin silicone spatula to release the edge of the omelet. While releasing the edge, tilt the pan slightly in the opposite direction.

When one side of the omelet is rolled toward the center, add the cheese and tomato. Continue rolling the omelet closed and onto a plate.

Brush with the remaining tablespoon of butter and sprinkle with bacon and oregano.

LORELAI: *"Not too many tomatoes."*

LUKE: *"Light on the tomatoes."*

LORELAI: *"Very light, just a teeny-tiny amount, practically none."*

LUKE: *"I'm skipping the tomatoes. It's an omelet with Jack cheese."*

LORELAI: *"Perfect!"*

FLUFFY
Buttermilk Pancakes

When your morning mugs of coffee aren't enough to fill you, whip up a batch of pancakes as a yummy side dish to your caffeine. A bestseller at Luke's Diner, these extra fluffy buttermilk pancakes go fast, so you have to order quickly before they sell out! Or beg and beg and beg until you wear Luke down, and he puts some aside for you. Dress them up with blueberries, chocolate chips, and whipped cream, or your favorite flavored syrup.

YIELD: About ten 5-inch pancakes

1½ cups all-purpose flour

¾ teaspoon baking soda

1½ teaspoons baking powder

2 tablespoons granulated sugar

¼ teaspoon fine sea salt

1¾ cups buttermilk, plus more as needed

2 large eggs

3 tablespoons unsalted butter, melted, plus butter for serving

1 cup blueberries

1 cup mini chocolate chips

Canola oil, for cooking

Pure maple syrup, for serving

Whip cream for serving, optional

FOR LEMON MAPLE SYRUP

1 cup maple syrup

Zest of 1 lemon

Juice of 1 lemon

FOR COFFEE MAPLE SYRUP

1½ teaspoons instant coffee

1½ teaspoons hot water

1 cup of maple syrup

Preheat the oven to 200°F. In a large bowl, sift together the flour, baking soda, baking powder, sugar, and salt.

In a medium bowl, whisk together the buttermilk, eggs, and melted butter. Pour the buttermilk mixture into the flour mixture and stir just until combined.

Place a griddle over high heat until hot. (To test, flick a little water onto the griddle. It should skitter across the surface.) Lightly oil the griddle. For each pancake, pour about ¼ cup of the batter onto the griddle and cook until bubbles form on the surface, about 2 minutes. If adding blueberries or chocolate chips, sprinkle on during these 2 minutes. Flip the pancakes and cook until the bottoms are golden brown, 1 to 2 minutes more. Transfer to a baking sheet and keep warm in the oven.

Repeat until all the batter is used. If the batter begins to thicken, thin it with a bit more buttermilk.

Serve the pancakes piping hot, with plenty of butter and syrup. Garnish with any leftover blueberries or chocolate chips.

PUT A SPIN ON IT
To dress up the maple syrup—and enjoy a double dose of berries—in a small saucepan, gently simmer 2 cups blueberries with 1 cup pure maple syrup until the berries start to release their juices, about 5 minutes.

LEMON SYRUP
In a heatproof bowl, combine the maple syrup, lemon zest, and lemon juice and warm for 30 seconds at a time in the microwave—stirring in between, heat for 1 minute total. Alternatively, combine ingredients in a small saucepan, over medium low heat, and bring to a gentle simmer. Serve immediately.

COFFEE SYRUP
Combine the hot water and instant coffee together and stir until the coffee is dissolved. Combine the coffee mixture and the maple syrup in a heatproof bowl and warm for 30 seconds at a time in the microwave—stirring in between, heat for 1 minute total. Alternatively, combine in a small saucepan, over medium low heat, and bring to a gentle simmer. Serve immediately.

"I'm gonna have pancakes with a side of pancakes."

LORELAI

CLASSIC
Luke's Diner Cheeseburger

In times of turmoil, or joy, or when you're starving, or just a little bit hungry, nothing hits the spot like a Classic Luke's Diner Cheeseburger. These juicy, flavorful burgers are served between a warm toasted bun. Luke himself warns that red meat can kill, but it's okay to splurge sometimes for dinner or lunch, or for breakfast, or maybe a midnight snack, or anytime you're bored.

YIELD: 4 burgers

FOR THE PATTIES
1½ pounds ground beef chuck
½ teaspoon garlic powder
Kosher salt and freshly ground pepper
Olive oil, for brushing
4 slices Cheddar cheese

FOR ASSEMBLY
Hamburger buns, preferably from a local bakery, split and toasted
Sliced red onion and sliced tomato, for serving
Mayonnaise, ketchup, or mustard, for serving

In a medium bowl, combine the ground beef, garlic powder, and ½ teaspoon pepper. Using a fork, stir it together, keeping the mixture crumbly rather than compressed.

With a light hand, form 4 loosely packed patties, and then gently flatten each patty to about ½-inch thick. Refrigerate the patties for 15 minutes.

Warm a large, heavy sauté pan, griddle, or frying pan over high heat until it is very hot, 2 to 3 minutes. Reduce the heat to medium-high, brush the tops of the patties with oil, and season generously with salt. Place the patties in the pan, oiled side down, and cook, without moving them, for 3 minutes. Brush the tops of the patties with oil, season generously with salt, and turn.

Continue to cook 5 to 7 minutes more, until an instant-read thermometer inserted into a burger registers 140° F for medium, or to your desired doneness. Add a slice of cheese to the top of each patty during the last 2 minutes of cooking and let it melt.

Assemble according to taste and condiment choices.

"I would like a cheeseburger, with a side of cheeseburger, and see if they can make me a cheeseburger smoothie."

LORELAI

LORELAI: *"I brought you a wimpy with a rose pinned on it."*

LUKE: *"A what?"*

LORELAI: *"A turkey burger with onions."*

LUKE'S
Health-Conscious
Turkey Burger

Luke's been trying to nudge Lorelai and Rory toward a healthier lifestyle for years—more "vegetables" and less "blowing their brain cells out with coffee"—with no success. When his daughter April shows up, he finally has a kindred spirit with whom to share his healthier meals. This zesty turkey burger is a noble first step on the road to health-conscious living. Luke serves it with sweet potato fries and broccoli, but if that goes against everything you believe in, add a side of Chili Cheese Fries (page 26).

YIELD: 4 burgers

FOR THE PATTIES
½ cup Greek yogurt
1 tablespoon Dijon mustard
1 teaspoon dried chives
1 pound ground turkey
½ teaspoon salt
¼ teaspoon garlic powder
¼ teaspoon smoked paprika
Fresh ground pepper to taste
Vegetable oil, for brushing

FOR ASSEMBLY
4 whole wheat hamburger buns
4 slices red onion
1 avocado, sliced
4 slices of Monterey Jack cheese, optional
Reserved yogurt spread

TIP: A cast-iron griddle works best for this. If you don't have a cast-iron griddle, make sure to use a pan that can take high heat.

In a small bowl, combine the Greek yogurt, Dijon mustard, and dried chives and set aside.

In a medium mixing bowl, combine the ground turkey, salt, garlic powder, paprika, and pepper and fold in half the yogurt mixture. Refrigerate the remaining yogurt mixture and use as a bun spread.

Form the meat into 4 equal patties, place on a plate or cookie sheet, and chill in the refrigerator for 15 minutes.

When ready to cook, heat the griddle on high and brush with vegetable oil.

Place the patties on the oiled griddle and let cook undisturbed for 4 to 6 minutes until well browned and easy to flip. Cook on the other side for another 4 to 6 minutes. Add cheese slices at this point, if using. An instant-read thermometer should read 165° F.

Remove the patties to a plate to rest. Toast the buns on the griddle.

To assemble, split the remaining yogurt mixture between each bun bottom. Top each bottom with a patty. Place a slice of onion and 2 or 3 slices of avocado on each top and serve open-faced to let guests add additional condiments like ketchup or mustard. Serve with sweet potato fries.

SANTA
Burger

Bah, hamburger! If ever there was proof that Luke's Scrooge persona is just an act, it's the Santa Burger he whips up when Lorelai is desperate for some yuletide cheer. This festive favorite starts with one of Luke's famous juicy burgers and is finished off with a few unusual toppings: lots of cream cheese, a cherry tomato nose, and one extra-special secret ingredient. (SPOILER: It's love! The extra-special secret ingredient is love!)

YIELD: 4 burgers

1 pound ground beef chuck

½ teaspoon garlic powder

½ teaspoon freshly ground pepper

2 tablespoons olive oil, plus more for brushing

Kosher salt

1 red bell pepper, cut in half, seeded

1½ cups shredded Monterey Jack cheese

8-ounce block of cream cheese, softened

4 hamburger buns, preferably from a local bakery, split and toasted

1 white onion, sliced

FOR FACE GARNISH:

8 jalapeno slices

4 cherry tomatoes

4 long pickle slices, cut in half

In a medium bowl, combine the ground beef, garlic powder, and ½ teaspoon pepper. Using a fork, stir it together, keeping the mixture crumbly rather than compressed.

With a light hand, form 4 loosely packed patties, then gently flatten each patty to about ½ inch thick. Refrigerate the patties for 15 minutes.

Preheat the oven to 400°F.

Place the bell pepper halves on a rimmed roasting tray, coat lightly with olive oil, and sprinkle with salt. Roast for 15 to 20 minutes until skins are blistered and peppers are soft. Immediately transfer to an airtight container, cover, and let stand for 5 to 10 minutes, or until cool enough to handle. Remove the skins and cut each half in half, creating hat-shaped pieces. Reserve scraps.

Warm a large, heavy sauté pan or griddle over high heat until it is very hot, 2 to 3 minutes. Reduce the heat to medium-high, brush the tops of the patties with oil, and season generously with salt. Place the patties in the pan, oiled side down, and cook, without moving them, for 3 minutes. Brush the tops of the patties with oil, season generously with salt, and turn. Continue to cook 5 to 7 minutes more, until an instant-read thermometer inserted into a burger registers 140°F for medium, or to your desired doneness.

In a small bowl with a fork mix together shredded Monterey Jack and cream cheese until well blended.

To assemble, place a burger patty on a bottom bun with your desired condiment. Spread a thick layer of cheese mixture on the top bun and place directly next to the burger patty. Use a little bit more cream cheese mixture to join the two pieces together and create Santa's mustache. Add reserved pepper pieces for his lips, a cherry tomato for his nose, and jalapeno slices for his eyes. To make the hat, lay the pepper piece just at the top of the burger patty and prop up with stacked pickle pieces. Use a center onion piece and a dollop of cream cheese as his pom-pom. Place onion pieces cut in half for his eyebrows, just above the jalapeno slices.

TIP: FAT IS FINE! For the best flavor and juicy texture, you want your ground beef to have about 20 percent fat. When making burgers, don't opt for the lean beef. It's time to splurge!

"He has a hat and everything!... No one has ever made me something quite this disgusting before. I thank you!"

LORELAI

CHILI CHEESE
Fries

Luke doesn't approve of this artery-clogging dish (really, what *does* Luke approve of?), but he begrudgingly serves up this diner favorite anyhow. Salty, spicy, and savory all at once, these Chili Cheese Fries are a hearty holdover until your next snack. Make your own potato fries while the chili simmers on the stove.

YIELD: 4 servings

FOR THE CHILI
1 tablespoon neutral cooking oil
1 large red onion, chopped
4 cloves garlic, chopped
3 jalapenos, seeded and chopped
1½ pounds ground beef
3 tablespoons chili powder
1 tablespoon chipotle powder
2 teaspoons ground cumin
1 teaspoon smoked paprika
1 teaspoon cayenne pepper
One 14-ounce can diced tomatoes
One 14-ounce can kidney beans
1 cup beef broth

FOR THE FRIES
2 pounds large potatoes, such as russet
Neutral oil for frying
Salt
2 cups prepared chili
2 cups shredded Cheddar cheese
Sour cream, for garnish, optional
Sliced scallions, for garnish, optional

To make the chili, in a large pot, heat the oil over medium heat. Add the onion and cook until lightly browned, about 5 minutes, and then add the garlic and jalapenos and cook for 2 more minutes, until they are starting to soften.

Add the beef and brown for about 5 minutes; then add the chili powder, chipotle powder, cumin, paprika, cayenne, tomatoes, kidney beans, and beef broth and bring to a boil.

Lower the heat to a simmer and cook for about 40 minutes, until the chili has thickened and the flavors are melded. Remove from the heat.

To make the fries, peel the potatoes, if desired. Cut each potato into thin slices about ¼ inch thick and then cut each slice into sticks. Soak in cold water for at least 2 hours, or overnight.

Preheat the oven to 350°F. Drain the potatoes and dry with paper towels.

Heat 2 inches of oil to 300°F in a large skillet or Dutch oven. Fry the potatoes in batches until golden brown, 2 to 3 minutes, and remove to paper towels to drain.

Transfer the fries to an oven-safe platter and then top with the chili and cheese. Bake until the cheese is melted, 8 to 10 minutes.

Top with sour cream and scallions, if using.

"I need something with cheese."

LORELAI

CAESAR'S
Salad

Salad lovers (bleh) probably know the classic Caesar's salad ingredients by heart: onion, guacamole, butter lettuce. Not what you were expecting? You were probably thinking of the Caesar salad. That's something totally different—there's no apostrophe S in that one. This recipe includes a homemade dressing, fresh guacamole, and more greens than Lorelai eats in an entire year.

YIELD: 4 main servings or 6 side servings

FOR THE DRESSING
½ cup avocado oil
3 tablespoons apple cider vinegar
Juice of ½ lime
½ teaspoon salt
½ teaspoon coriander
Fresh black pepper to taste
⅛ to ¼ teaspoon red pepper flakes, depending on desired spice level

FOR THE GUACAMOLE
4 ripe avocados
Juice of ½ lime
1 teaspoon salt
1 serrano pepper, cut in half, deseeded, and finely diced
½ cup diced cherry tomatoes
½ cup finely diced red onion
½ cup freshly chopped cilantro leaves
Fresh ground pepper to taste
For the salad assembly:
2 heads butter lettuce, leaves separated, washed, and dried
1 cup cherry tomatoes, cut in half
Half a red onion, thinly sliced and then sliced in half to create ribbons

To make the dressing, combine the avocado oil, apple cider vinegar, lime juice, salt, coriander, black pepper, and red pepper in a jar with a tight-fitting lid. Set aside until needed.

To make the guacamole, cut the avocados in half, remove the pits, and scoop the flesh into a medium bowl. Add the lime juice and salt and use a fork to smash the avocado and incorporate. Keep some of the avocado chunky, do not overwork.

Add the serrano pepper, tomatoes, red onion, and cilantro, and gently fold in. Add fresh ground pepper to taste. Cover with a lid or plastic wrap and set aside.

If you are individually plating the salads, reserve some of the larger lettuce leaves to line the salad bowls. In a large salad bowl, tear the lettuce into bite-sized pieces. Add the cherry tomatoes, red onion, and enough dressing to coat. Extra dressing can be refrigerated in an airtight container for up to 1 week for future use.

To plate, line four salad bowls with 2 or 3 whole butter lettuce leaves. Fill the center with a quarter of the dressed salad, and top with a scoop of guacamole.

LANE: *"There's already a Caesar salad. It's kind of famous."*
CAESAR: *"That's Caesar salad. Mine's got an apostrophe S."*

DELICIOUS
Donuts

Donuts: the perfect food. Often loaded with fillings, frostings, and candy, this magnificent dessert has for some unknown reason been designated as a breakfast food, but it's been Gilmore-approved for any meal, activity, or crisis. If you're a purist, stick with the basic recipe, but if you're not Emily Gilmore, go wild and add some fun finishes like a chocolate glaze or cinnamon sugar or speckle with Froot Loops.

YIELD: About 15 donuts and their holes

FOR THE DOUGH
¾ cup whole milk

3 tablespoons unsalted butter

3¼ cups all-purpose flour, divided

⅓ cup granulated sugar

½ teaspoon salt

2½ teaspoons quick-rise yeast

2 large eggs

½ teaspoon vanilla extract

Canola or peanut oil, for brushing and deep-frying

FOR THE VANILLA GLAZE
6 tablespoons unsalted butter, melted

2½ cups powdered sugar

1 teaspoon vanilla extract

5 tablespoons hot water, plus more as needed

FOR THE CHOCOLATE GLAZE
3 tablespoons unsalted butter, melted

1¼ cups powdered sugar

¼ dark unsweetened cocoa powder

2 to 4 tablespoons hot water, plus more as needed

CINNAMON SUGAR
¼ cup sugar

½ tablespoon cinnamon

To make the dough, in a small saucepan over medium heat, combine the milk and butter and heat, stirring, until the butter is melted and the mixture is hot but not boiling (about 125°F on an instant-read thermometer). Remove from the heat.

Fit a stand mixer with the paddle attachment. In the mixing bowl, combine 2½ cups of the flour, the sugar, salt, and yeast and beat on low speed to mix. Add the hot milk mixture, raise the speed to medium, and beat until well blended. Add the eggs and vanilla and beat until fully incorporated, about 2 minutes. Add the remaining ¾ cup flour and beat until the dough is well blended and smooth, about 1 minute longer. The dough will not pull away from the sides of the bowl and will still be somewhat sticky.

Line a baking sheet with waxed paper and brush the paper with oil. Line a second baking sheet with paper towels. On a generously floured work surface, roll out the dough into a circle 10 inches in diameter and ½-inch thick. Using a 3-inch round donut cutter, cut out as many donuts as possible. Transfer the donuts and holes to the oiled paper. Gather up the donut scraps and repeat rolling and cutting. Cover the donuts and holes with a clean kitchen towel and let rise until soft and puffy, about 30 minutes.

Pour oil to a depth of 2 inches into a deep-fryer or deep, heavy sauté pan and warm over medium-high heat until it reads 360°F on a deep-frying thermometer. Carefully lower 2 to 5 donuts or holes into the hot oil and deep-fry until dark golden, about 1½ minutes. Turn the donuts over and cook until dark golden on the second side, about 1 minute longer. Transfer to the towel-lined baking sheet. Repeat to fry the remaining donuts and holes, allowing the oil to return to 360°F between batches.

To make the vanilla glaze, in a small bowl, whisk together the melted butter, powdered sugar, vanilla, and hot water until smooth. Whisk in 1 to 2 teaspoons more hot water if needed to give the glaze a thin, light consistency. Use right away.

When the donuts and holes are cool enough to handle but still warm, dip all sides in the vanilla glaze, letting any excess glaze drip back into the bowl. (You may not use all of the glaze, but this makes for easier dipping.) Place on a wire rack and let stand until the glaze sets, about 30 minutes.

To make the chocolate glaze, in a small bowl whisk together the cocoa powder and hot water. Add the melted butter and powdered sugar; continue to whisk until the glaze is smooth and shiny. Add more hot water if the glaze is too thick.

For the chocolate glaze, dip just the top half of the donut and rest on a wire rack until set. Donut holes can also be served with warm chocolate glaze as a dip.

For cinnamon sugar donuts or donut holes, glaze the donut or hole with the vanilla glaze, roll in cinnamon sugar, and place on rack to set.

Arrange the donuts on a platter and serve right away.

MIXING WITH A FOOD PROCESSOR: If you do not have a stand mixer, you can use a food processor with fine results: Following the sequence outlined in the recipe, add the dry ingredients to the work bowl and pulse 3 or 4 times to mix. Add the liquid ingredients and process for 20 to 30 seconds to form a dough. Transfer the dough to a bowl or a work surface, according to the recipe, and proceed as directed.

CHICKEN NOODLE SOUP
With a Side of
Mashed Potatoes

According to Luke, the best way for Lorelai to get rid of her cold is to have a healthy immune system, and the best way to get a healthy immune system is to eat vegetables. But last time we checked, Luke's not a doctor, so what does he know? Lorelai's preferred sick food is a hot hearty bowl of chicken noodle soup with a side of creamy mashed potatoes. Feel free to pick out the carrots if they offend you.

CHICKEN NOODLE SOUP

YIELD: 8 servings

2 tablespoons olive oil

3 medium yellow onions, diced

4 cloves garlic, minced

4 large carrots, diced

4 large celery stalks, diced

1 teaspoon salt

1 teaspoon pepper

1 teaspoon dried dill

12 cups vegetable broth

4 cups chicken bone broth

4 cups shredded cooked chicken, preferably from a roasted chicken

1½ cups bow tie pasta

In a large stockpot over medium heat, heat the olive oil and then add the onions and garlic. Cook until the onions are translucent, about 10 minutes. Add the carrots and celery and cook another 10 minutes.

Add the salt, pepper, dill, stock, vegetable broth, chicken broth, and chicken. Bring to a simmer and cook for 10 minutes. Add the pasta and simmer another 10 minutes. Serve hot.

"It's the third day in a row you've ordered soup for breakfast.... At least eat the carrots in the soup this time, not just the noodles."

LUKE

"Alright, pancakes, one fried egg, side of bacon. Chicken noodle soup, side of mashed potatoes."

LUKE

MASHED POTATOES

YIELD: 6 to 8 servings

4 large Yukon Gold potatoes, about 2 pounds

2 tablespoons Kosher salt

3 large cloves garlic

½ cup whole milk

½ cup sour cream

2 tablespoons unsalted butter

Additional salt and pepper to taste

Peel and quarter the potatoes. Fill a large saucepan about three-quarters full of water, add 2 tablespoons salt, and then add the potatoes and garlic. Bring to a boil, reduce the heat to low, and simmer, uncovered, until the potatoes are tender when pierced with the tip of a paring knife, about 30 minutes. Drain the potatoes.

Place the potatoes in a large bowl and use a potato masher or a large fork to mash them to the desired texture. Cover the bowl with a kitchen towel to keep warm.

In a small saucepan over medium heat, combine the milk, sour cream, and butter and bring the mixture to just below a boil. Immediately remove from the heat. Gradually add the milk mixture to the potatoes while stirring with a fork. The potatoes should be smooth and thick. Beat the potatoes a few times with a large spoon to smooth them out. Season with salt and pepper and serve immediately with Chicken Noodle Soup (page 30).

TIP: Need to make these ahead? Spread them into a large casserole dish, cover, and refrigerate. To serve, preheat the oven to 375°F, uncover the potatoes, and dot with 2 tablespoons unsalted butter. Bake for 45 minutes to an hour or until heated through and golden brown on top.

DANISH DAY
Danishes

Nothing's worse than getting in a Sid-and-Nancy caliber fight with Luke right before Danish Day. When Lorelai oversteps between Luke and Jess, she and Luke end up in a big blowout, and Luke refuses to let Rory sneak a second Danish for her. Next time Luke is withholding when she's hungry, even Lorelai can handle this recipe using sweet apple, cherry, or raspberry filling and a store-bought dough. Or she could, if she knew how to use all those little knobs on her oven.

YIELD: 12 Danishes

One 17-ounce package puff pastry, thawed according to package directions

8 ounces of cream cheese, softened

1 tablespoon lemon juice

¼ cup powdered sugar

1 teaspoon vanilla paste

1 egg yolk, egg white reserved for egg wash

1 recipe apple or cherry filling (page 123), optional as filling

1 cup fresh raspberries, optional as filling

Prepare two cookie sheets with silicone baking mats or parchment paper.

Roll puff pastry out to a 10-by-15-inch rectangle, keeping the edges as straight as possible. Cut into six 5-by-5-inch squares. Repeat with the second piece of pastry. Chill while you make the cheese filling.

In a medium bowl, combine the cream cheese, lemon juice, egg yolk, powdered sugar, and vanilla paste. Use a hand mixer to beat until smooth. Set aside.

In a small bowl, make the egg wash by adding 1 tablespoon of water to the egg white and whisking until frothy.

Working with half the pastry squares at a time, and in the center of a square, place a mounded tablespoon of cream cheese filling. Use a pastry brush to brush egg wash on the corners. Fold each corner of the pastry to the center and press down gently.

If using apple filling, take a square of pastry, add egg wash to the edges and fold in each side about ¾ inch to create a box. Fill the center with about 2 tablespoons of apple filling.

If using fresh raspberries, create the box, fill with about 1 tablespoon of cheese filling and top with 3 to 4 fresh raspberries.

Refrigerate pastries while preheating the oven to 425°F.

When the oven is heated, brush egg wash on the top of each pastry and bake for 20 to 25 minutes, or until puffed and golden brown. Transfer to wire rack to cool.

Glaze if desired by mixing ½ cup powdered sugar with 1 teaspoon lemon juice, and 2 teaspoons dairy milk. Drizzle over Danishes when almost cool.

"...What better day to make up than Danish Day, the happiest of all days. The day when we all say, 'Hey, let's forgive and forget over a nice Danish and a cup coffee.'"

RORY

"I don't have many people in my life who are in my life permanently, forever. They will always be there for me. I will always be there for them. You know? There's Rory and Sookie, this town, and you."

LORELAI

PERFECT
Peach Pie

Who says nobody ever eats the peach pie? Weston's Bakery offers Luke some stiff competition in the pie department, so if he's going to sell pie, it has to be perfect. To bake the Perfect Peach Pie, first one must render the perfect peaches, so follow the Sookie St. James rules for purveying the perfect peach: Small means watery, and watery means no good peach taste. Watery peaches roll differently, so when in doubt, roll them peach by peach across the kitchen floor.

YIELD: 1 Pie

FOR THE PIE CRUST
2½ cups all-purpose flour

2 teaspoons powdered sugar

1 teaspoon salt

½ cup plus 2 tablespoons unsalted butter, very cold, divided

¼ cup solid vegetable shortening, very cold

⅓ cup ice water

FOR THE FILLING
5 cups peaches (about 4 to 6 peaches), fresh or frozen

½ cup plus 1 tablespoon sugar, divided

½ teaspoon ground ginger

Pinch of ground clove, optional

4 tablespoons tapioca flour or starch

Juice of 1 lemon (about 3 to 4 tablespoons)

2 tablespoons milk (any dairy variety will work)

Preheat the oven to 425°F.

To make the pie crust, in a large bowl, combine the flour, sugar, and salt together. Cut ½ cup of the cold butter and the shortening into small pieces. Using a pastry cutter or two forks, work the butter into the flour mixture until all of the pieces are pea-sized or smaller.

Add the ice water a little bit at a time and use the pastry cutter to bring the dough together. As the dough starts to come together, switch to your hands or a spatula, using up to ½ cup of water, until the dough just comes together.

Split the dough in half, turn out onto a floured surface, and roll out into a round that extends past your 9-inch pie dish. Trim the edge of the dough so that it extends only about ¼ inch past the edge of the pie dish.

Repeat with the second piece of dough; then fold it in fourths and place inside the pie dish. Refrigerate while you prepare the fruit.

If using fresh peaches, peel and slice them.

To make the filling, mix the peaches, ½ cup sugar, ginger, clove (if using), tapioca flour, and lemon juice together. If using fresh fruit, let stand for 10 minutes. If using frozen, do this just before the filling goes into the pie dish.

Fill the pie dish with the fruit mixture and dot with two tablespoons of butter. Place the top crust on top, fold over the bottom edge, and pleat using your fingers. Vent the pie crust by snipping, with kitchen shears or a paring knife, two lines to make an X into the top. Brush with the milk and sprinkle with 1 tablespoon of sugar.

Bake for 45 minutes to an hour until the crust is golden and fruit is tender. You should see the fruit bubbling through the vent. Allow to cool completely on a wire rack for the cleanest cut. Serve with whipped cream.

CAESAR'S
Chilaquiles!

Chilaquiles! Caesar insisted that patrons of Luke's Diner would go nuts for these fried tortillas, and, boy, was he right! This tasty Mexican dish is full of rich flavors. Chilaquiles! The garlic and peppers, cotija cheese, savory sauce, and fried tortillas will have your mouth watering and begging for more. Chilaquiles!

YIELD: 6 servings

Two 28-ounce cans whole tomatoes

3 cloves garlic, smashed and peeled

2 teaspoons salt, plus more for tortillas

1 serrano chile or jalapeno, stemmed

Sixteen 8-inch corn tortillas

1 quart oil, for frying

6 eggs, fried to order

Crumbled cotija cheese, for garnish (optional)

Sliced avocado, for garnish (optional)

Add the tomatoes, garlic, salt, and whole chile to a medium saucepan on high heat. Bring to a low boil, then reduce heat, and simmer until garlic and chile are very soft, about 30 minutes.

Use an immersion blender to blend the sauce until it's smooth. If you don't have an immersion blender, let sauce cool enough to safely blend in a countertop blender. (You may need to do this in batches.)

Cut the tortillas like a pie, into sixteenths. Prepare your frying station (see page 166 for notes) and heat the oil to 365°F. Fry the tortillas in small batches. Remove and drain on a paper towel, lightly salting while still hot.

To assemble: Heat ½ cup of sauce in a large sauté pan on medium. Add 2 handfuls of tortilla chips to the pan, and simmer until chips are tender but not soggy. Transfer chips to a plate, and top with a fried egg. Add avocado and cheese, if desired.

Want a shortcut? You can use store-bought corn chips! But be careful: They will become soggy much faster than freshly fried tortillas.

"Chilaquiles, huh? . . . People went nuts for them. Mr. and Mrs. Fiss said they want them every morning now. Who knew? I didn't even think we'd sell one of them."

Zach

CHAPTER Two

The Independence Inn, The Dragonfly Inn, & Sookie St. James's Creations

Sookie St. James is more than just the consummate best friend: She's a talented, passionate, dare we say magical gourmet chef. Sure, she's kind of klutzy, and her kitchen has seen plenty of dropped pots and minor to major injuries, but her decadent dishes have mouths watering all over Stars Hollow.

Whether it's cooking for friends, for her catering company, for the Independence Inn (until the entire place burned down), or for the Dragonfly Inn (except during that short period after she set the stove on fire), Sookie puts all of her love into the food she creates. She makes hearty soups! Delightful canapes! Cakes in the shape of hats! Put it this way: Even Emily Gilmore is impressed by Sookie's cooking.

ROQUEFORT
Puffs

These tasty treats are the perfect hors d'oeuvre for any town-wide event in Stars Hollow, whether it's a wedding, in celebration of Rory being in the top 3 percent of her class, or the wake of a 206-year-old cat. How good are these puffs? They're so good Luke even let Sookie garnish his meatloaf with them. This recipe makes a puff that's light, flaky, and filled with tangy Roquefort cheese.

YIELD: 24 puffs

One 14-ounce package puff pastry, thawed according to package directions

3 ounces Roquefort / blue cheese crumble, softened

2 ounces unsalted butter, softened

½ teaspoon freshly ground black pepper

2 teaspoons minced fresh thyme

1 egg whisked with 1 tablespoon of water, for egg wash

SPECIAL EQUIPMENT

Square or round cookie cutters, about 2 inches and 1 inch

If necessary, roll out puff pastry until ¼-inch thick. Transfer the dough to a cookie sheet lined with a silicone baking mat. Line a second cookie sheet and set aside.

Use the large cookie cutter to cut out pairs of dough. Use the smaller cookie cutter to cut a window in half the pieces. Reserve the small centerpiece. Refrigerate while preparing filling.

To prepare the filling, place the cheese, butter, black pepper, and thyme in a small bowl and mash and blend with a fork until everything is incorporated. Small chunks of cheese are okay. Place filling in a piping bag and snip off about ½ inch from the end.

Remove the cookie sheet from the refrigerator. Use a pastry brush to brush the egg wash over the bottom pieces of each puff. Top each puff with a window piece, setting it at an angle to make a diamond. Fill the center window with a 2-teaspoon mound of cheese filling and top with the small center piece of dough, pressing down gently.

When all the puffs are filled, freeze for at least 1 hour. At this time, the puffs can be placed in an airtight container with parchment paper in between the layers. Keep frozen until ready to serve.

When ready to serve, preheat the oven to 425°F and bake for 15 to 20 minutes until puffed up and golden brown. Serve hot. Leftovers can be stored in an airtight container for a day or two but will lose their crisp soon.

"Roquefort puffs would complement that dish quite well!"

SOOKIE

JACKSON'S
Blueberry Shortcake

This Stars Hollow specialty is a stellar substitute when the produce guy only has substandard strawberries. Jackson's Blueberry Shortcake bursts with flavor from plump, ripe blueberries. Since the recipe makes a pound cake rather than standard shortcake biscuits, it yields plenty of servings, so you can be sure to have some "used cake" to bring to your next Friday Night dinner.

YIELD: 10 to 12 servings

FOR THE CAKE

3 cups all-purpose flour, plus more for preparing the baking pan
½ teaspoon baking soda
2 teaspoons baking powder
1 cup (2 sticks) butter, room temperature, plus more for greasing the baking pan
2 cups sugar
4 eggs
½ cup whole milk
2 teaspoons vanilla paste
1 cup sour cream

FOR THE BLUEBERRIES

5 cups blueberries, rinsed, divided
2 lemons, zest removed and set aside
1 cup sugar, divided

FOR THE WHIPPED CREAM

1½ cups heavy whipping cream
3 tablespoons powdered sugar

Whisk the flour, baking soda, and baking powder together in a medium bowl and set aside.

In the bowl of a stand mixer, beat the butter until light and fluffy, slowly add the sugar, and continue beating until pale in color and all the sugar is incorporated. Add the eggs one at a time, beating after each addition until incorporated.

In a small bowl, whisk together the milk, vanilla, and sour cream until combined but not necessarily smooth.

Alternate adding the flour mixture and sour cream mixture to the butter mixture, ending with sour cream and beating on low after each addition until incorporated.

Butter and flour the bottom only of a 9-by-13-inch baking pan. Add the cake batter to the baking pan and bake for 40 to 45 minutes or until a cake tester comes out clean. Remove cake from the oven and poke holes across the surface. Allow to cool.

Combine one cup of blueberries, juice of 1 lemon, and ½ cup of sugar in a small saucepan over medium-high heat. Bring to a boil and boil 3 to 5 minutes until most of the blueberries have broken down and the mixture is slightly thickened. Remove from heat and allow to cool slightly, about 5 minutes. Strain out blueberry pulp and reserve the syrup, discarding the pulp; pour the syrup over the cake. Use a pastry brush to spread the syrup around and make sure that it covers the whole surface. The syrup will soak into the cake while you prepare the berries and whip cream.

In a large bowl, mix the lemon zest with remaining ½ cup of sugar, the juice of the remaining lemon, and the remaining 4 cups of blueberries. Set aside and allow to macerate.

Just before serving, prepare the whipped cream by combining the heavy whipping cream and powdered sugar in the bowl of a stand mixer and mixing on high until soft peaks form.

To serve, cut squares of the cake, pile blueberries on top or alongside, and top with a generous dollop of whipped cream.

NOTE: This cake can be made a day ahead and kept refrigerated. The blueberries can macerate for up to 3 hours in the refrigerator but should be brought up to room temperature before serving.

JACKSON: *"Use the blueberries."*

SOOKIE: *"To make what?"*

JACKSON: *"Blueberry shortcake."*

SOOKIE: *"There's no such thing!"*

INDEPENDENCE INN

SOOKIE'S
Magic Risotto

(Most) critics agree that Sookie's Magic Risotto is out-of-this-world delicious. With flavors so tantalizing it's been known to coax people's mothers back from death's doorway, this risotto packs a punch with shrimp, scallops, and saffron. It's better than fine—it's magical, enchanting, bewitching, breathtaking. Just be sure to pair it with the right wine!

YIELD: 6 servings

½ pound (25 to 30) shrimp, with shells

4 cups vegetable broth

2 cups water

3 cloves garlic, peeled and smashed lightly

1 teaspoon kosher salt

6 stalks parsley, leaves, and stems separated

½ teaspoon saffron threads

1 pound sea scallops

2 tablespoons olive oil, divided

3 tablespoons unsalted butter, divided

1 small shallot, thinly sliced

2 cups uncooked risotto rice

¾ cup dry white wine (one you enjoy drinking)

Peel and devein the shrimp. Reserve the shells and chop the shrimp into bite-sized pieces. Refrigerate the shrimp in an airtight container.

In a large saucepan combine the vegetable broth, water, garlic cloves, salt, shrimp shells, and parsley stems. Bring to a low boil over medium-high heat. Then remove from heat, cover, and let stand for 15 minutes.

Strain the broth through a fine mesh strainer into a large bowl or measuring cup and discard all solids.

Return the empty saucepan to the stove over medium heat and allow to dry out for 30 seconds to a minute. Add the saffron threads and toast, stirring continually for 30 seconds to 1 minute.

Return broth to the saucepan and bring back to a simmer. Remove from heat and cover to keep warm.

Lay the scallops out on several layers of paper towels and pat dry.

In a large sauté pan big enough to hold the scallops in a single layer, heat 1 tablespoon olive oil and 1 tablespoon butter over medium-high heat.

When the butter has foamed, place the scallops in a single layer and leave undisturbed for 1 minute.

After 1 minute, use tongs to gently flip each scallop. Cook for another 30 seconds to 1 minute, remove to a plate, and set aside.

Add an additional 1 tablespoon of olive oil to the pan and sauté the shallots until they just start to brown, 3 to 5 minutes. Then add the rice and sauté until translucent around the edges. Add the wine and stir until it has been absorbed.

Add the warm broth one ladleful at a time until absorbed between each ladleful. After adding about ¾ of the broth, add the chopped shrimp.

Continue adding broth until the final ladleful. With the final ladle, add the scallops and the remaining butter. Serve in low bowls, with 2 to 3 scallops on top, a scattering of chopped parsley leaves, and a glass of the rest of your white wine.

SOOKIE'S
Wedding Cake & Cupcakes

As if Sookie doesn't have enough to worry about in the days leading up to her wedding—choosing a perfect, non-morbid song to walk down the aisle to, swapping out all the Jordan almonds for aspirin, Jackson's last-minute skirt change—Stars Hollow's resident chef also makes her own wedding cake. This tower of cupcakes is iced with a buttercream frosting, garnished with beautiful edible flowers, and sits beneath a tiny wedding cake perfect for the happy couple to share on their big day.

YIELD: One 2-tier, 4-inch cake and about 20 cupcakes

FOR THE CAKE BATTER
3 eggs

1 cup whole milk

Zest of 1 small orange

2 tablespoons fresh orange juice

1 teaspoon vanilla paste or vanilla extract

2¼ cups all-purpose flour

1¼ cups sugar

4 teaspoons baking powder

¼ teaspoon salt

¾ cup (1½ sticks) salted butter, softened

FOR THE FROSTING
1/3 cup water

2 tablespoons meringue powder

6 cups sifted powdered sugar, divided

¾ cup unsalted butter, softened

½ tablespoon vanilla extract

½ teaspoon almond extract

½ teaspoon salt

1 to 2 drops orange essential oil, optional

FOR DECORATING
Food coloring

Edible flowers

Herbs such as mint or lavender

Pastry bags and tips, such as round and leaf

Pallet knives and or offset spatulas

Line a standard cupcake pan with paper liners of your choice and grease a 6-inch cake pan. Preheat the oven to 350°F.

To make the cake batter, whisk the eggs in a medium bowl. Add the milk, orange zest, orange juice, and vanilla. Set aside.

In the bowl of a stand mixer with paddle attachment (or in a large mixing bowl using a hand mixer), combine the flour, sugar, baking powder, and salt. Stir until combined. Add the softened butter, stirring on low until a coarse crumb mixture forms.

Reserve ½ cup of the egg mixture and add the rest to the batter bowl. Mix on medium (or high if using hand mixer) for about 2 minutes. Stop the mixer, add the remaining ½ cup egg mixture, and beat for 1 minute more. Stop the mixer again, scrape down the sides of the bowl, and mix about 30 seconds more. Scoop batter into the cupcake liners, filling ¾ of the way full and fill the 6-inch cake pan. Bake cake for 25 to 30 minutes or until a cake tester comes out clean and bake the cupcakes for 15 to 20 minutes.

Continues on page 48

"I went with the sugared daffodils for the top tier. Let me tell you, they look great. Ooh, I've outdone myself this time."

SOOKIE

Continued from page 47

To make the frosting, in the bowl of a stand mixer fitted with a whisk attachment, combine the water and meringue powder. Whip on high until soft peaks form. Add 4 cups of the sugar, 1 cup at a time, beating on low after each addition. Alternate the remaining sugar with a few tablespoons of butter at a time, mixing on low after each addition. When all the sugar and butter is incorporated, mix in the vanilla extract, almond extract, essential oil, if using, and salt. Continue to beat on low until smooth. Use immediately or store in an airtight container, refrigerated, for up to two weeks.

NOTE: If refrigerated, frosting must be brought to room temperature before using.

To decorate the cake and cupcakes, start by slicing the cake into two equal layers. Fill and frost completely in frosting. Use an offset spatula to frost each cupcake with a flat layer of frosting. Once all the cupcakes and the cake have been frosted white, put them in the refrigerator for at least 20 minutes while you color the rest of the frosting. Choose your palette, making sure you have a good mix of dark and light colors and at least 1 green for leaves.

Once the cake and cupcakes have chilled, you can begin decorating. The frosting flowers photographed were created by frosting large dots or lines and then "spreading" them into petal shapes with a small offset or palette knife. Alternatively, some flowers were created by spreading a thin layer of frosting on a baking mat and using a palette knife to "gather" frosting, like you would oil paint, and placing it on the cupcakes as a petal. Each additional petal lays against the first. The edible flowers and herbs were used to decorate additional cupcakes, as a cake topper, and to fill in between cupcakes on the tower.

DEEP-FRIED
Turkey Leg

Deep frying a beautiful organic Thanksgiving bird might seem blasphemous to a professional chef, but that didn't stop Jackson and his family from deep frying their turkey . . . and their vegetables, mashed potatoes, cake, and various non-food related items (deep-fried napkins, anyone?). Fried turkey is a little unorthodox for Thanksgiving, but we promise the crispy outcome is worth it. If the mere thought of this still stresses you out, turn to Sookie's Survival Margaritas (page 54) for support.

YIELD: 4 to 6 servings

24 cups water

4 cups kosher salt

3 bay leaves

1 bulb of garlic, halved, crosswise, no peeling necessary

1 tablespoon black peppercorns

½ tablespoon coriander seeds

8 cups ice

4 pounds turkey drumsticks and/or thighs

6 tablespoons unsalted butter, softened

SPECIAL TOOLS

About 2 quarts of frying oil such as canola, peanut, or safflower

Deep fryer or very large pot

RORY: *"It's too much food."*

LORELAI: *"It's not. This is what we've been training for our whole lives. This is our destiny. This is our finest hour."*

RORY: *"Or final hour."*

In a very large pot, big enough to hold 2 gallons of water and the turkey meat, combine 12 cups of water, salt, bay leaves, garlic, peppercorns, and coriander seeds. Bring to a boil, and cook until all the salt is dissolved. Remove from heat, and add 12 more cups of water and the ice, and allow to cool completely.

When the brine is completely cool, add the turkey legs and/or thighs. If necessary, place a plate directly over the legs and thighs in the brine to weigh them down (you want to make sure they remain completely submerged throughout the brining process). Alternatively, you can transfer both the brine and turkey to a large, resealable bag. Place the pot (or bag, if using) in the refrigerator, and allow the turkey to brine for 4 hours. After 4 hours, remove the turkey from the brine, pat dry, and set aside while preheating the oven. Discard the brine.

ROASTING INSTRUCTIONS
Preheat the oven to 450°F.

Place a baking rack inside a rimmed baking sheet, arrange the turkey pieces on the rack, and rub the turkey all over with the butter. Roast for 30 minutes. Reduce the heat to 325°F, and baste the turkey with the butter and juices. Roast another 15 minutes before checking the internal temperature. Remove the turkey from the oven when it has reached 165°F. Tent with foil and allow to rest for 20 minutes. The temperature will continue to rise as it rests. Serve hot, and feel free to enjoy on the go.

FRYING INSTRUCTIONS
Fill the fryer to its minimum oil level or fill the pot so that the oil is about 3 inches deep. You want to make sure that there will be plenty of room for the oil to bubble and rise when the turkey legs are added. Bring the oil up to 350°F. Gently lower 1 leg at a time into the oil and cook until the internal temperature reaches 165°F, 12 to 15 minutes. Turn to brown on all sides.

MEDIEVAL FEAST
Plum Pudding

The Independence Inn is known for throwing elaborate events, but none were quite as elaborate as the Bracebridge dinner. If you're planning your own authentic 19th century dinner with peacock pies, men dressed as squires, sleigh rides that definitely lean more romantic than platonic, and Kirk in a blouse, a mouthwatering plum pudding is the perfect way to top off the night—but an authentic plum pudding requires a year to "settle." You can use this more modern plum clafoutis recipe if you didn't plan tonight's menu a year in advance.

YIELD: 8 to 10 servings

FOR PLUM VERSION
1 tablespoon butter, for greasing
3 to 4 ripe plums, sliced
⅛ teaspoon ground cloves
¾ cup plus ½ tablespoon sugar
3 eggs
¾ cup all-purpose flour
¾ cup whole milk
2 teaspoons vanilla paste, divided
1 tablespoon port
Pinch of salt
¼ cup heavy cream
1 teaspoon powdered sugar

FOR PRUNE VERSION
8 ounces (about 2 cups) pitted prunes
2 tablespoons port
1/8 teaspoon ground cloves
Enough boiling water to cover prunes

SPECIAL TOOLS
10-inch pie dish

Preheat oven to 375°F.

Grease the bottom of the pie dish with butter. Lay the plums in concentric circles around the bottom of the pie plate, layering if necessary.

Combine the cloves and ½ tablespoon of sugar. Sprinkle over the plums.

In a medium bowl, beat together the eggs and ¾ cup of sugar until light and frothy, about 2 minutes. Add in the flour and beat on low until smooth.

In a separate bowl, combine the milk, 1½ teaspoons vanilla paste, port, and pinch of salt. Pour into the flour and egg mixture and stir to combine. Pour over the fruit and bake for 10 minutes. Reduce oven to 350°F and bake another 20 to 25 minutes, or until the cake tester comes out clean. Allow to cool on a wire rack.

To make the whipped cream, in a medium bowl combine the heavy cream, powdered sugar, and remaining ½ teaspoon vanilla paste, and whisk or beat with a hand mixer until soft peaks form.

Serve the pie warm with sweetened whipped cream.

Plums not in season? Want to be extra medieval? Swap for prunes.

Combine the prunes, port, and cloves. Add enough boiling water to just cover the prunes and soak for 15 minutes. Drain and discard liquid. Place the prunes in the bottom of the baking pan and proceed with batter as above.

"Fresh fruit has such sensuality."

MISS PATTY

SOOKIE'S
Critically Acclaimed
Zucchini Soup

The opening of the Dragonfly Inn is a stressful time because Lorelai wants everything to be perfect, including the menu. And a perfect menu has to include Sookie's Critically Acclaimed Zucchini Soup, a smooth vegetable soup accompanied by a zingy gremolata. The key to this delicious recipe is perfect, fresh zucchinis, so if your perfect, fresh zucchinis are facing the threat of a potential cold front coming in from Canada? You sleep with the zucchinis.

YIELD: 6 servings

FOR THE SOUP

3 tablespoons olive oil, divided

3 zucchinis (about 1½ pounds total), cut into ½-inch cubes, divided

4 to 6 cloves of garlic, minced

Salt

3 leeks (about 1½ pounds total), thinly sliced, white and light green parts only

1 celery rib, finely chopped

8 cups vegetable broth

1 russet potato, peeled and diced

1 lemon

Freshly ground pepper

FOR THE BASIL OIL

1 cup loosely packed basil leaves

½ cup loosely packed flat parsley leaves

Juice of ½ lemon

½ cup good quality olive oil

Pinch of salt to taste

In a large, heavy pot, heat 1½ tablespoons of the oil over high heat. Add about half of the zucchini and spread in a single layer. Cook, without stirring, until beginning to brown, about 1½ minutes. Stir and then cook, stirring occasionally, until the zucchini is just tender, about 2 minutes. Stir in half of the garlic and ¼ teaspoon salt and cook until fragrant, about 30 seconds. Transfer to a large plate.

Add the remaining 1½ tablespoons oil to the pot and heat over medium-high heat. Add the leeks, celery, remaining garlic, and ¼ teaspoon salt and stir to mix well. Reduce the heat to low, cover, and cook, stirring occasionally, until the leeks soften, about 10 minutes. Add the broth, potato, and remaining zucchini, raise the heat to high, and bring to a boil. Reduce the heat to low, cover partially, and simmer, stirring occasionally, until the potato is tender, about 15 minutes. Add back in browned zucchini. Use an immersion blender to puree the soup until smooth. Finely zest the lemon with a microplane and stir into soup. Add fresh black pepper to taste.

To make the basil oil, in the bowl of a food processor or blender, add the basil and parsley and pulse to chop. Add the lemon juice and pulse again to break down into a paste. While the processor is running, slowly add the olive oil and puree until the mixture is smooth. Add salt to taste.

To serve the soup, ladle into a bowl and drizzle with basil oil.

SOOKIE: *"Davey's with his grandparents and Jackson's sleeping with the zucchini tonight."*

LORELAI: *"What's that, farm jargon?"*

SOOKIE'S
Survival Margaritas

Amateurs ambushing your kitchen? Serve up a pitcher of Sookie's Survival Margaritas, and you'll soon forget about the culinary crimes taking place. This recipe makes a refreshing limeade that you can also kick up with an alcoholic twist. If you go that route, add the ice, then add one ounce of orange-infused tequila before adding the juices. Let these potent potables guide you through the five stages of grief, on the rocks with salt.

YIELD: 4 servings

FOR THE INFUSED TEQUILA
One 750-milliliter bottle of blanco (white or silver) tequila
1 large navel orange, rinsed well and cut in half

FOR THE LIMEADE
1½ cup fresh lime juice from 8 to 10 limes
40 ounces of limeade
1 to 2 pinches of kosher salt
Zest of 1 orange

FOR THE MARGARITAS
2 cups Infused Tequila, optional Ice
Lime wedges for garnish

SPECIAL SUPPLIES
Large bottle or jar
Skewers

To make the Infused Tequila, preheat the oven to 425°F.

Place the orange cut-side up on a baking sheet. Roast for 20 to 30 minutes, until it is blistered and caramelized. Remove from the oven and allow to cool.

In a container large enough to hold both the oranges and tequila, decant the tequila and submerge the oranges, using skewers to help keep them submerged. Let the tequila infuse for at least 6 hours (if infusing for longer, transfer to the refrigerator after 6 hours). Strain the tequila through a fine-mesh strainer, into a sealable container, and refrigerate until needed.

To create the limeade, stir the fresh lime juice into the limeade, add the salt to taste, and the zest of the orange. Allow limeade to infuse at least 2 hours before serving. To serve as a mocktail, pour limeade over ice and garnish with a lime wedge.

To make the margaritas, in a large pitcher add the 2 cups of tequila and then top off with limeade. Chill for at least 1 hour and then serve over ice and garnish with a lime wedge.

"I've already gone through the five stages of grieving: Denial, anger . . . I don't remember these two, but they were served on the rocks with salt!"

Sookie

JALAPEÑO-CHIPOTLE
Mac & Cheese

With Sookie's cooking and Lorelai's charisma, starting a catering business seems like a great way for Lorelai and Sookie to make some money before the Dragonfly Inn opens—until they cater a kids' birthday party. If you're trying to keep a big group of children happy, you can't go wrong with macaroni and cheese! Unless you make a PG-13 version with jalapeño peppers. The spicy flavors in this mac will have kids in tears from the first big, unexpectedly flaming bite, but it's perfectly palatable for an adult get-together.

YIELD: 6 servings

2 tablespoons unsalted butter, plus butter for the baking dish

Kosher salt

¾ pound dried elbow macaroni

3 cups milk

1 to 2 jalapeño chiles, seeded and chopped

¼ teaspoon red pepper flakes (optional)

2 tablespoons all-purpose flour

1 pound pepper jack or Monterey jack cheese, shredded, divided

Preheat the oven to 375°F. Butter a 2-quart baking dish. Fill a large pot three-quarters full of salted water. Bring water to a boil over high heat. Add the macaroni, stir well, and cook until al dente, according to the package directions. Drain the pasta and set aside.

Meanwhile, in a saucepan, combine the milk and chiles, and pepper flakes, if using, and warm over medium heat until small bubbles appear along the sides of the pan. Remove from the heat and let sit for 10 to 25 minutes, depending on the desired heat level, tasting often. Strain the milk, reserving the chiles and the milk.

In a large saucepan, melt the butter over medium heat. Whisk in the flour and 1½ teaspoons salt and cook, whisking constantly, until the flour smells toasted, about 1 minute. Slowly add the milk, ¼ cup at a time, while whisking constantly to break up any lumps. When all the milk is incorporated, continue to whisk until the mixture thickens slightly, about 3 minutes.

Reserving 2 cups for the top, add the cheese, a handful at time and stir each time until smooth. Toss the cheese sauce with the pasta and transfer to the prepared baking dish and sprinkle with the remaining cheese and the reserved chiles. Bake until bubbling and browned on top, about 30 minutes. Let sit for a few minutes before serving.

LORELAI: *"It's green. Why is it green?"*

SOOKIE: *"Because I made it with a jalapeño-chipotle cream sauce."*

LORELAI: *"Kids aren't gonna eat this."*

LOBSTER
Bisque

Chef Sookie's lobster bisque is as rich as a Chilton kid on their trust fund birthday. Make your own stock from two whole lobsters as a base for the sweet, creamy bisque. Food critic Lucent Mills, though dangerously uneducated when it comes to risotto, was right when he said that this bisque is worth every sinful, cream-filled rich sip.

YIELD: 8 to 10 servings

FOR THE STOCK

5 tablespoons unsalted butter

2 tablespoons olive oil

4 carrots, scrubbed and roughly chopped

2 stalks celery, roughly chopped

4 cloves garlic, peeled and roughly chopped

¼ cup brandy

4 tablespoons tomato paste

2 cooked lobsters, meat removed and set aside, carcasses and tomalley for stock

6 stalks of parsley, stem only, leaves reserved

1 teaspoon kosher salt

½ teaspoon whole peppercorns

2 bay leaves

8 cups vegetable broth

½ cup cream

FOR THE ROUX

8 tablespoons unsalted butter

½ cup flour

1 lemon, for serving

In a large Dutch oven or soup pot over medium-high heat, melt the butter in the olive oil. When the butter begins to foam, add carrots, celery, and garlic. Stir to coat and continue to sauté until vegetables begin to brown and are fragrant, 5 to 8 minutes.

Deglaze the pot with brandy and cook for 2 to 3 minutes. Add tomato paste and cook 2 to 3 minutes more.

Add the lobster carcasses, parsley stems, salt, peppercorns, bay leaves, and vegetable broth to the pot. Add as much water as is needed to cover the lobster shells. Bring to a boil and then reduce to a simmer. Simmer partly covered for 1 hour.

For the roux, melt the butter in a pan on medium-low, add the flour, and stir almost continuously until the mixture reaches a deep caramel color.

NOTE: This can be done ahead while the stock is simmering and could take up to 8 minutes.

Strain the broth through a fine mesh strainer lined with cheesecloth into a large heatproof container. Put the broth back into the pot, add the roux, and bring to a gentle simmer. Add the cream.

Chop the reserved parsley leaves and combine with the zest of 1 lemon in a small bowl.

In a medium skillet, heat the 3 tablespoons of butter until just melted, add the reserved lobster meat, and cook for 1 to 2 minutes.

To serve, place a few pieces of lobster in the bottom of each bowl, sprinkle with the parsley lemon zest mixture. Ladle the soup of the lobster meat and serve.

NOTE: If serving with Lobster Pot Pie (page 146), reserve the tail meat for the pot pies.

"Her lobster bisque is worth every sinful cream-filled rich sip."

LUCENT MILLS, FOOD CRITIC

LORELAI'S
Graduation Cake

What do you get for the graduate who has everything? How about a megadose of caffeine? When Lorelai graduates from community college, Sookie creates an elaborate cake in the shape of a graduation hat. Filled with chocolate covered espresso beans, this cake will wake you right up after a long stretch of late-night studying for finals.

YIELD: Serves 8 to 10

FOR THE CAKE BATTER

1½ cups sugar

1 ⅓ cups all-purpose flour

⅔ cup unsweetened cocoa powder

½ teaspoon salt

1¼ teaspoons baking powder

1¼ teaspoons baking soda

2 eggs

½ cup milk

1½ teaspoons vanilla paste or vanilla extract

6 tablespoons salted butter, melted

¾ cup hot brewed coffee

FOR THE FROSTING

½ cup (1 stick) unsalted butter, softened

8 ounces cream cheese, softened

2 cups powdered sugar

¼ cup unsweetened cocoa powder

10 ounces bittersweet chocolate, melted

1 tablespoon instant coffee

¼ cup hot water

½ cup mascarpone cheese

A few drops black food coloring

About 1 pound chocolate-covered espresso beans or chocolate candy of choice

SPECIAL SUPPLIES

Two 6-inch cake pans

1 ovenproof bowl with approximately a 6-inch diameter at the mouth

10-by-10-inch black cardstock

2½ yards white ribbon

Preheat the oven to 350°F.

To make the cake batter, sift together the sugar, flour, cocoa powder, salt, baking powder, and baking soda. Transfer to the bowl of a stand mixer with a whisk attachment (or use a hand mixer in a medium bowl) and blend briefly.

In a separate bowl, whisk together the eggs, milk, vanilla, and melted butter until well combined.

Add wet ingredients to dry and mix on low for 3 minutes. Slowly add the hot coffee and mix on low until just combined. Make sure to scrape the bottom of the bowl (batter will be very thin).

Cut parchment to line the cake pan bottoms. Spray the ovenproof bowl with non-stick cooking spray and cut 2 strips of parchment, long enough to fit all the way across the bottom of the bowl and stick out either side. Place them in the bowl like an X.

Pour the batter into the cake pans and bowl. Bake the cakes for 20 to 25 minutes or until a cake tester comes out with a few moist crumbs.

When you remove the cakes from the oven, allow them to cool on a wire rack for 15 minutes. Run an offset spatula around the edges of the two cake pan cakes, and use a cooling rack to invert the cake pans and remove the cakes. Allow to cool completely. For the bowl cake, after 15 minutes use your fingers to gently press an indent into the center of the cake, about 3 inches wide and deep. Put the cake in the freezer until ready to frost.

Continues on page 60

LORELAI: *"Aw, you made me a tassel hat cake!"*

SOOKIE: *"Filled with two pounds of crushed chocolate-covered espresso beans."*

LORELAI: *"You're evil."*

Continued from page 59

To make the frosting, in the bowl of a stand mixer, with a paddle attachment, beat the butter and cream cheese together until light and fluffy. In a small bowl, mix the powdered sugar and cocoa. Add the sugar mixture to the butter mix on low, about a ½ cup at a time, until incorporated. Add in the melted chocolate a little at a time and beat on low after each addition.

In a small bowl, mix the instant coffee and hot water together until the coffee dissolves.

Add the mascarpone cheese to the butter mix on low to incorporate and then add the coffee and mix again. With the mixer on medium high, mix for 30 seconds to 1 minute, until smooth. Add food coloring and mix again. Note black frosting darkens over time.

To assemble: Have a cake stand or serving plate standing by. Use an offset spatula and the parchment strips to remove the cake from the bowl. Place the bowl-shaped cake on a cutting board.

Using a cookie cutter, or a glass, cut a 3-inch circle from the center of 1 of the 6-inch cakes. Frost the "cake ring" with a layer of frosting and carefully place it on top of the cake bowl, frosting side down, to adhere.

Fill the cavity with the chocolate-covered espresso beans or candy, but reserve at least 4 beans or pieces of candy.

Frost the top of the second cake layer around the edges but avoid the center. Invert the second cake layer, lining it up with the edges of the first, and sealing the cavity. At this point chill the cake for 20 minutes.

When the cake has chilled, gently move it to the cake stand, inverting it so the bowl-shaped cake becomes the top. Frost completely.

To make the mortarboard top, cut a piece of stiff, black cardstock into a 10-by-10-inch square. Use about 2½ yards of white yarn to make the tassel. Starting at one end of the yarn piece, wrap your 4 fingers over and over, 10 times. Pull the looped yarn off your fingers and about an inch down from 1 end, wrap yarn around 4 to 5 times and tie off. This creates the top of the tassel. Use scissors to cup open the looped ends at the other end of the tassel. Use glue to attach the tassel to the cardstock. Place the reserved candy pieces at 4 "corners" of the top of the cake and rest the cardstock on top. This will keep the cardstock from pulling frosting off the top of the cake.

CIABATTA BUN
Caprese Sandwiches

The most talented chef in all of Stars Hollow and beyond doesn't need a *stove* to make a delicious meal—which is a good thing, because when the stove catches fire at the Dragonfly Inn, it takes a few days to get it up and running again. But have no fear, culinary extraordinaire Sookie St. James saves the day with a cold no-stove-needed spread, including these caprese sandwiches on ciabatta buns. Use large ripe heirloom tomatoes to get the fullest flavor.

YIELD: 4 sandwiches

½ cup balsamic vinegar

1 tablespoon honey

3 tablespoons good quality olive oil, divided

4 ciabatta buns, split in half

2 cloves garlic, peeled and smashed gently

2 cups loosely packed baby arugula leaves

1 cup loosely packed basil leaves, chiffonade

1 teaspoon salt, divided

2 large heirloom tomatoes

Fresh black pepper to taste

8 ounces fresh mozzarella, sliced

8 thin slices of prosciutto (about 3 ounces), optional

In a small saucepan, add the balsamic vinegar and honey and cook over medium-low heat, stirring frequently. Continue to cook until mixture is reduced by about a third and it coats the back of your spoon. Remove from heat and allow to cool. Note: This could take 10 to 15 minutes to reduce and 20 plus minutes to cool. It can be done a day or two ahead and stored in a squeezy bottle or airtight container and refrigerated until needed.

After the glaze is cooled, preheat the oven to 350°F.

Use 2 tablespoons of the olive oil to brush both sides of each ciabatta bun and place on a cookie sheet. Rub each side of the buns with the garlic cloves. Discard garlic or reserve for another time.

Toss the arugula, basil, remaining 1 tablespoon of olive oil, and ½ teaspoon salt together in a bowl and set aside.

When the oven is hot, toast the buns, olive oil side up, for 5 minutes, flip and toast another 3 to 5 minutes.

While the buns are toasting, slice the tomatoes into thin slices and arrange on a plate and sprinkle with fresh ground pepper to taste and with the remaining ½ teaspoon salt.

To assemble each sandwich, place a small handful of the arugula mix on the bottom bun, top with 1 slice of tomato, a slice of mozzarella, then another slice each of tomato and mozzarella. If using, fold two pieces of prosciutto on top and follow with a garnish of additional arugula mix. Cover with the top bun pieces and slice in half on the angle. Note: This can also be set up as a sandwich building station.

SOOKIE'S
Roasted Acorn Squash Soup

Sure, Sookie and Jackson have a beautiful love story, but the love story between Sookie and gourds is one for the ages. After one hot summer in Stars Hollow, the squash crop runneth over into the Dragonfly Inn kitchen, leaving Sookie with all the acorn squash she needs to make her roasted acorn squash halves. Filled with squash soup, these sweet, rich meals are basically pie in soup form. Try to do *that* with zucchini tushes.

YIELD: 8 servings

FOR THE SOUP

4 large acorn squash, halved and seeded and the bottom trimmed so they sit level

1½ tablespoons olive oil, divided

1 teaspoon salt

1 tablespoon butter

1 shallot, finely minced

1 sprig rosemary

⅓ cup white wine

1½ cups vegetable broth, plus more as desired

Fresh black pepper to taste

FOR TOPPING

1 tablespoon unsalted butter

½ cup raw pumpkin seeds

½ teaspoon paprika

Dried cranberries, optional

Creme fraiche, for garnish, optional

Preheat the oven to 450°F.

Place the acorn squash halves on rimmed baking sheets and rub the interiors with about ½ tablespoon olive oil and salt. Bake for 30 to 40 minutes until the squash flesh is just tender, but the sides are not collapsing.

Allow the squash to cool until you can comfortably handle. Gently scrape the flesh from the interiors of the squash bowls. Be careful to leave enough flesh to keep the bowl standing, about ¼ inch. Set flesh aside and reserve squash shells for serving.

Heat a large Dutch oven on medium-high heat and add the remaining olive oil and butter. When the butter begins to foam, add the shallot and sauté until fragrant, about 2 or 3 minutes. Add the sprig of rosemary and the white wine, deglaze the pan, and cook for 3 to 4 minutes to cook off the alcohol.

Add in the roasted squash pieces and the broth and simmer for 15 to 20 minutes, until the squash is falling apart. Add fresh black pepper to taste.

Remove the rosemary sprig and use an immersion blender to puree the soup until smooth. Adjust the seasoning, reduce to low and keep warm until serving.

To make the topping, melt the butter in a small skillet over medium-low heat and add the pumpkin seeds, paprika, and cranberries, if using. Stir until the pumpkin seeds are toasted and well coated. Transfer to a plate to cool.

To serve, place each roasted acorn squash half in a shallow soup bowl and fill with soup. Sprinkle about a tablespoon of the pumpkin seed mixture in the middle and drizzle with the crème fraiche.

"Jackson's whole squash crop went crazy this year. We had such a hot summer, and these babies love the sun. You've got to try this soup."

Sookie

NORMAN MAILER'S
Legendary
Iced Tea

Norman Mailer, UGH! Best known for ruining lunch at the Dragonfly Inn (Sookie's ONE THING), this renowned writer is often found loitering in the Dragonfly dining room midday, taking up space, using big words, not eating food, and ordering pitcher after pitcher of iced tea. What's so great about iced tea anyway? It's cold, refreshing, sweet with just the right amount of lemon—okay fine, maybe Norman's on to something here.

YIELD: 6 to 8 servings

FOR THE TEA

3 tablespoons loose-leaf English breakfast tea

1 tablespoon loose-leaf hibiscus tea

6 cups boiling water

Large tea infuser, optional

FOR THE SIMPLE SYRUP

1 lemon

1 cup sugar

1 cup water

3-inch piece of ginger peeled and cut up into chunks

FOR SERVING

Ice

Lemon wedges

To make the tea, place the loose-leaf teas in a tea infuser. In a large heatproof container, mix the English breakfast tea, hibiscus tea, and boiling water. Steep for 4 to 6 minutes to desired strength. Keep in mind you want a strong brew since it will dilute with ice.

After the tea has steeped, if not using a tea infuser, strain out the tea leaves and refrigerate the tea for 4 to 6 hours before serving.

To make the simple syrup, use a vegetable peeler or paring knife to remove the zest of the lemon, being careful not to include the pith, in long strips.

In a small saucepan, bring the sugar, water, ginger, and lemon zest to a boil.

Remove from heat and allow to cool completely. When syrup is cool, strain zest and ginger from the syrup. Store syrup in an airtight container and refrigerate until needed.

When ready to serve, fill a large serving pitcher with ice, pour tea over the ice, and sweeten with the syrup by adding about ¼ cup or to desired sweetness. Alternatively, you can serve the syrup alongside the tea and let guests sweeten themselves. Serve with a big bowl of lemon wedges.

"And I'm thrilled and delighted that Norman Mailer is coming in here every day and sitting at a table for four and ordering nothing at all, but tea!"

SOOKIE

" *I live in*
TWO
WORLDS:
one is a
WORLD
of
BOOKS. "

— *Rory*

BROCCOLI
Tarts

Lorelai has her reservations when her mother hires her and Sookie to cater Richard and Jason's launch party. After all, nobody is pickier than Emily Gilmore. Emily makes them jump through hoops to get the job—and then ends up firing them after Jason convinces Richard to cancel the party and take the clients on a trip to Atlantic City instead. This led to some feelings of fierce filial loyalty from Lorelai, a date with Jason, and a house filled with hundreds of leftover broccoli tarts.

YIELD: 72 tarts

12 ounces frozen broccoli florets

3 cloves garlic

3 ounces Manchego cheese, cut into small ½-inch chunks

½ cup pine nuts, toasted

1½ teaspoons lemon juice

1½ teaspoons kosher salt

¼ cup mascarpone cheese

9 sheets filo pastry, defrosted according to package directions

½ cup unsalted butter, melted

SPECIAL TOOLS

2½ inch square cookie cutter or pastry wheel

Mini muffin pans

Pastry brush

Bring a large pot of salted water to a boil and have an ice bath standing by. Blanch the broccoli for 2 minutes (for tips on blanching vegetables, see page 166). Drain and immediately plunge into the ice bath. Allow to cool in the ice bath for 1 minute before draining again. Press broccoli to remove as much moisture as possible.

In the bowl of a food processor, add the following ingredients one at a time and pulse between additions: garlic, broccoli, Manchego cheese, pine nuts, lemon juice, salt, and mascarpone. After the mascarpone has been added, the mixture should come together like a soft dough.

Preheat the oven to 350°F.

Working on a large cutting board, lay down 1 sheet of filo pastry and brush all over with butter. Add 2 more layers of pastry, brushing each one with butter to make three layers.

Have the mini muffin pan and the filling standing by. Use the cookie cutter to cut through all three layers of pastry. Alternatively, you can measure out 2½-inch marks along both edges of the dough and cut squares out with a pastry wheel. Keep the remaining filo covered with a damp kitchen towel because it dries out quickly. Place each dough square over an opening in the muffin tin and press down gently.

Place a scant 1 tablespoon of filling in the center of each tart shell. Repeat until all the muffin cups are filled.

Cut the remaining squares of dough into strips and separate into ribbons with your fingers. Top each tart with a couple of ribbons.

Bake for 8 to 10 minutes or until the filo is golden brown and crisp.

When the first batch is cool, 5 to 7 minutes, remove them to a serving tray or store in an airtight container.

While the first batch of tarts are baking, repeat the process with three more sheets of filo to create a second filled muffin pan.

Bake for 8 to 10 minutes or until the filo is golden brown and crisp.

Using the last three sheets of filo, repeat the process for the final round of tarts.

HANDKERCHIEF PASTA
With Brown Butter Sauce

Fall in New England is cozy, and fall in Stars Hollow is even cozier, and fall at the Independence Inn is a living, breathing Norman Rockwell painting. This silky handkerchief pasta with a brown butter sauce, the very entree that sent food critic Lucent Mills through the roof, feels like a warm sweater and a skinny scarf on a brisk autumn day.

YIELD: About 1 pound of dough

FOR THE PASTA DOUGH
2 cups "00" flour, divided

Pinch of kosher salt

¼ cup dried porcini mushrooms, pulverized in a food processor

2 tablespoons fresh thyme leaves, minced

2 large eggs plus 2 large egg yolks

1 tablespoon olive oil

1 tablespoon water

FOR THE BROWN BUTTER SAUCE
8 tablespoons good quality unsalted butter

Juice of half a lemon

Salt and pepper to taste

To make the pasta by hand, place the flour on a work surface, mix in the salt, mushroom, and thyme, shape into a mound. Make a well in the center. Add the eggs, egg yolks, oil, and water to the well. Using a fork, beat until blended, keeping the liquid inside the well. Continue to gently beat the egg mixture, gradually drawing in the flour from the sides of the well. When the mixture is too stiff to use the fork, gently mix the dough with your fingertips, gradually drawing in more flour just until a soft, moist, but not sticky ball of dough forms. Leave any remaining flour behind by using a bench scraper, to clean the work surface. Dust the work surface with flour and knead the dough until smooth and elastic, about 10 minutes.

To make the pasta with a stand mixer, in the bowl fitted with the paddle attachment, mix 1½ cups of the flour, mushroom, thyme, and salt. In a liquid measuring cup, whisk together the eggs, egg yolks, oil, and water. Slowly drizzle the egg mixture into the flour, beating on medium speed until combined, about 1 minute. Turn the dough out onto a lightly floured surface and knead by hand until smooth and firm, adding more flour as needed, about 4 minutes.

Allow the gluten in the dough to relax before rolling. Place the dough made by any method on a lightly floured work surface, cover with a kitchen towel, and let rest for 30 minutes, or wrap in plastic and refrigerate for up to 2 days; if refrigerated, let the dough stand at room temperature for 30 minutes before using.

To make the pasta in a food processor, in the processor bowl, combine 1½ cups flour and salt and pulse to mix. In a liquid measuring cup, whisk together the eggs, egg yolks, oil, and water. With the processor running, add the egg mixture in a steady stream and process until combined and the dough forms small clumps that resemble coarse sand; the dough should not form a ball. Stop the machine and pinch the dough; it should come together when pinched but not be sticky. Turn the dough out onto a lightly floured surface and knead by hand until smooth and firm, adding more flour as needed, about 2 minutes.

"The entrees are as heavenly as the starters. Though the much lauded risotto was perfectly fine, it was the simple handkerchief pasta with brown sage in a butter sauce that sent me through the roof."

To use a manual pasta machine, set the rollers to the widest setting. Divide the dough into 3 equal pieces. Using your hands or a rolling pin, flatten the dough to about ¼ inch so that it will fit through the widest setting. Guide the dough through the rollers. Fold the ends of the pasta sheet over the center like a letter and pass it through the widest setting again, dusting with flour as needed to prevent sticking. Fold and roll the dough again until the dough is silky smooth, 3 to 4 times.

Switch to the next-thinnest setting and guide the dough through once. Repeat at each setting in sequence, dusting with flour as needed, until the desired thinness is reached, 6 or 7 on most pasta machines. Dust with flour and let rest for 10 minutes before cutting. Cut into a 3-by-3-inch handkerchief and lay out and cover with a kitchen towel until ready to cook.

To use a pasta roller and cutter, attach the roller attachment to the stand mixer and set the rollers to the widest setting. Divide the dough into 3 equal pieces. Using your hands or a rolling pin, flatten the dough to about ¼ inch so that it will fit through the widest setting. With the stand mixer on medium-low speed, guide the dough through the rollers. Fold the ends of the pasta sheet over the center like a letter and pass it through the widest setting again, dusting with flour as needed to prevent sticking. Fold and roll the dough again until the dough is silky smooth, 3 to 4 times.

Switch to the next-thinnest setting and guide the dough through once. Repeat at each setting in sequence until you have reached the desired thinness, 6 or 7. Dust with flour as needed to prevent the dough from sticking. Cut into a 3-by-3-inch handkerchief and lay out and cover with a kitchen towel until ready to cook.

A pasta roller will help create the thinnest and silkiest pasta but patience and some elbow grease will work, too. After the dough has rested, work with about a third of the dough at a time. On a lightly floured surface, roll it out until it is about ¼-inch thick, fold it in thirds like a letter, and roll out again. Continue to roll the dough, rotating it to prevent sticking, until it is thin enough to see your hand through. Rest and cut as above.

For the brown butter sauce, in a large sauté pan over medium heat, melt the butter in the pan. Continue cooking the butter, stirring frequently, until it begins to brown and smells nutty, 7 to 10 minutes.

While the brown butter is cooking, bring a large pot of well-salted water to a boil. Cook the pasta for 1 to 2 minutes or until tender.

Remove the sauce from the heat and stir in the lemon juice. Add the salt and pepper to taste. Toss pasta in sauce and serve with shaved Parmesan cheese.

CHAPTER Three

A Stars Hollow Potluck

It's no wonder the Gilmore Girls are such Olympic-level eaters with all of Stars Hollow's food at their fingertips. There's Mrs. Kim's nutritious noshes, the variety of international cuisines at Al's Pancake World (but no pancakes!), the pancakes at Luke's, the tasty pies at Weston's when Lorelai and Rory are avoiding Luke, and Antolioni's when they're attempting to create the world's most giant pizza. Who can blame them for having a refrigerator that's empty but for a collection of takeout containers? And even when they're stuffed full with steak and way too many potatoes, there's always room for ice cream at Taylor's Olde Fashioned Soda Shoppe.

MRS. KIM'S
Eggless Egg Salad
Sandwiches

This Mrs. Kim staple had participants scrambling to keep dancing for twenty-four hours during the Stars Hollow Dance Marathon fundraiser. And it helped Dave Rygalski crack through Mrs. Kim's hard shell. And it sort of played a part in Jess poaching Rory from Dean. Wow, this egg salad has everything! Except eggs.

YIELD: 6 to 8 sandwiches

½ cup raw cashews

One 15-ounce can chickpeas, reserve the liquid for Aquafaba Dressing recipe (page 119)

½ teaspoon cumin

½ teaspoon turmeric

16 ounces silken tofu, gently pressed through paper towel or cheesecloth to drain

4 stalks green onion, white and light green parts, thinly sliced

½ cup finely chopped celery

Approximately ¼ cup Aquafaba Dressing (page 119)

Salt and freshly ground black pepper to taste

Loaf of sandwich bread and Dijon mustard, for serving

In a small saucepot, soak the cashews just covered in boiling water for 10 minutes. Strain the liquid from the cashews and discard. Roughly chop the cashews and add to a medium bowl. Set aside.

In a medium skillet over medium-high heat, combine the chickpeas, cumin, and turmeric and cook until the chickpeas are dry and begin to turn golden, 7 to 10 minutes. Remove from heat and use the back of a wooden spoon to gently smash the chickpeas. Allow to cool completely.

Add the drained tofu, green onions, celery, and cooled chickpeas to the bowl with the cashews and stir to combine.

Starting with about 2 tablespoons, add the Aquafaba Dressing until the "egg salad" has the desired consistency. Add salt and fresh ground pepper to taste.

To serve, toast bread before assembly if desired. Spread Dijon mustard lightly on each piece of bread. Spread about ½ cup of "egg salad" on to 1 piece of bread, top with a second piece, and slice in half. "Egg Salad" can also be served with crackers.

RORY: *"What stuff is that?"*

LANE: *"Eggless egg salad. Though this year my mom added food coloring to make the egg-like product look more eggy."*

RORY: *"Smart."*

MRS. KIM'S
Everything-Free
Muffin Drops & Tea

Given the obscene portion sizes of American cuisine, it can be tough to find a healthy and reasonable afternoon snack. This signature muffin drops recipe from Mrs. Kim is sugar-free, dairy-free, wheat-free, and rock 'n roll-free. Mrs. Kim's muffin drops need to be served with tea to make them soft enough to bite, but this version is edible on its own so the tea is a suggestion, not a requirement.

YIELD: About 18 muffin drops

2 cups whole pecans, divided

1 cup old-fashioned oats, gluten-free if preferred

1 cup pitted dates

3 very ripe bananas

½ teaspoon kosher salt

1 teaspoon vanilla bean paste

½ teaspoon cinnamon

SPECIAL SUPPLIES

1½-inch cookie scoop

Preheat the oven to 375°F. Prepare two cookie sheets by lining them with a silicone baking mat or parchment paper. Sort through the pecans and pull out 18 nice-looking ones. Reserve these for the tops of your muffin drops.

Heat a dry, medium-sized skillet on medium-high until very hot. Turn off the heat and add the remaining nuts to the pan. Toast the nuts, stirring gently, until fragrant, about 3 minutes.

Add oats to a food processor and pulse 2 or 3 times to create the base for your dough. Add dates and toasted pecans, and pulse a few more times, until the individual pieces are about the size of a pea. Add the bananas, and run the processor until the dough comes together, 1 minute or less.

Turn off the processor and scrape down the sides of the bowl. Add the salt, vanilla paste, and cinnamon and pulse until just combined.

Using the cookie scoop, scoop mounds of the dough on the prepared cookie sheets about 1 inch apart. Press a whole pecan into the top of each one. Bake for 15 to 20 minutes, or until the edges start to brown. Remove to a wire rack to cool—the drops will be soft but firm up as they cool. Serve immediately or store in an airtight container for 2 to 3 days.

"Tea is ready. I have muffins with no sugar, no dairy, no wheat. You have to soak them in tea to make them soft enough to bite, but they are very healthy."

MRS. KIM

MRS. KIM'S
Extra Chunky Multigrain Pudding

Apologizing isn't always easy, but there are other ways to say you're sorry. Mrs. Kim made her multigrain soy pudding as a peace offering, extra chunky just the way Lane likes it, to show her that she loves Lane, and she's sorry, and she accepts who Lane is. Wow. Who knew a chunky bowl of pudding could say so much? We used long-grained rice for this pudding and sweetened it with coconut cream and honey.

YIELD: 6 servings

2 cups water
Pinch of salt
1 cup long grain rice, such as Jasmine
1 cup walnut pieces, divided
2 cups unsweetened soy milk
½ cup honey
⅔ cup coconut cream
½ teaspoon allspice
½ cup black raisins
2 tablespoons flax seed

In a large saucepan, bring the water and pinch of salt to a boil. Add rice, stir, bring back to a boil, cover, and reduce to simmer. Cook rice for 15 minutes or until liquid has been absorbed.

While rice is cooking, heat a dry skillet over medium heat for 1 to 2 minutes, add ½ cup walnuts, and toast for 1 minute, stirring frequently. Remove from heat and allow walnuts to sit in hot pan 1 to 2 minutes more stirring occasionally until the nuts are fragrant. Set aside.

In a medium bowl, whisk the soy milk, honey, coconut cream, and allspice together. Set aside.

When rice is cooked, turn heat to medium-low and add the soy milk mixture. Continue to cook over medium to medium-low, stirring occasionally and making sure that rice does not stick to the bottom; cook-stir for 20 minutes.

At the 20-minute mark, add the remaining ½ cup walnuts, raisins, and flax seed. Continue to cook for another 10 to 15 minutes until most of the liquid has been absorbed and the mixture is a creamy porridge texture. Allow to cool for 5 minutes and then serve immediately with the toasted walnuts. Or refrigerate and eat cold.

LANE'S
Wedding Dumplings

When Lane and Zack get married, the residents of Stars Hollow, plus Lane's grandmother, attend their totally traditional Korean/Buddhist/Seventh Day Adventist wedding. This multigenerational event includes hidden crucifixes, mad dashes to the "real" ceremony in the church, tear-away wedding skirts, and yummy bartenders in disguise, all in the name of making mother and mother's mother happy. The wedding was capped off with these delicious dumplings packed with oyster mushrooms, bean sprouts, and tons of flavor. Add kimchi for some extra zip and serve with a spicy dipping sauce.

YIELD: About 50 dumplings

FOR THE DUMPLINGS
2 cups mung bean sprouts, rinsed
2 tablespoons vegetable oil, plus more for frying dumplings
2 teaspoons sesame oil, divided
½ yellow onion, finely chopped
2 cups oyster mushrooms
3 cloves garlic, minced
12 ounces extra firm or firm tofu
1 cup (about 1 bunch) green onions, thinly sliced
2 tablespoons soy sauce
½ cup kimchi, finely chopped, optional
50 round dumpling wrappers

FOR THE DIPPING SAUCE
4 tablespoons soy sauce
2 tablespoons rice vinegar
2 teaspoons chili sauce such as gochujang

Prepare a cookie sheet that can fit in the freezer with a silicone baking mat or parchment paper.

In a medium saucepot, bring 2 to 2½ cups of salted water to a boil. Boil the mung bean sprouts until tender, about 5 minutes. Drain and set aside.

In a large sauté pan over medium heat, heat the vegetable oil and 1 teaspoon sesame oil until it shimmers. Add the yellow onions and cook until just becoming translucent, 2 to 3 minutes. Add mushrooms and garlic and continue to cook until tender. Set aside.

Use cheesecloth or several layers of paper towel to drain the tofu cake by squeezing until most of the moisture has been released. Crumble and set aside.

In a large bowl, combine tofu, green onion, mung bean sprouts, and onion mushroom mixture. Add the remaining ½ teaspoon sesame oil and soy sauce, and mix thoroughly to combine.

Continues on page 81

MRS. KIM: *"You come down, cooking stops. Up."*

LANE: *"But it's hot up there mama, and you know what rises with the hot air? The smell of 10 pounds of Kimchi. I'm getting woozy."*

MRS. KIM: *"Well, pull your sweater over your face. Just get back upstairs."*

Continued from page 78

If using the kimchi, split the filling in half, approximately three cups each. Fold the kimchi into half of the filling and reserve. For a spicy dumpling option, fold in an alternate style such as pleated along the top.

On the center of a dumpling wrapper, place a heaping tablespoon of filling. Wet the edges all the way around the wrapper, fold in half, and seal closed, creating a half moon. Bring the ends together toward the center and pinch together to close. Alternatively, place a heaping tablespoon of filling in the middle of a wrapper and wet the edge of the wrapper all the way around. Bring the sides together, letting the filling create a flat bottom. Make the first pleat in the center of the dumpling and then continue to pleat on either side to finish.

After folding dumplings, place them on the prepared cookie sheet. Freeze all dumplings for at least 1 hour.

To make the dipping sauce, in a small bowl, whisk together the soy sauce, rice vinegar, and chili sauce and set aside. Refrigerate unused sauce in an airtight container.

Heat a large sauté pan with a tight-fitting lid over high heat. Coat the bottom with 1 to 2 tablespoons vegetable oil. When the oil starts to shimmer, place as many dumplings as can fit without touching in the pan. Let the bottoms brown for 3 to 4 minutes. Holding the lid of the pan at an angle to protect you from splatters, pour about a ¼ cup water quickly into the bottom of the pan and cover. Steam 3 to 5 minutes. Remove from heat and transfer to a platter. Repeat to finish remaining dumplings.

Alternatively, dumplings can be steamed in a bamboo steamer for about 5 minutes.

PASTA 3 WAYS
for Rory & Dean's
Three-Month Anniversary

Nothing says "I love you" (yikes!) like when Dean takes Rory to Antolioni's for their three-month anniversary and orders three different kinds of pasta when she can't choose. This dish includes a fettuccine alfredo you and your amore can slurp on for a romantic Lady and the Tramp moment, a penne with beef ragu, and a ziti with cheese sauce and beef ragu—because you shouldn't have to decide. See the pasta recipe on Handkerchief Pasta with Brown Butter Sauce (on page 70) to make homemade noodles, or use your own recipe.

BAKED ZITI

YIELD: 6 servings

1 pound ziti pasta
2 teaspoons salt
1 recipe Beef Ragu (page 85)
16 ounces fresh mozzarella cheese
½ cup Parmesan cheese

Preheat the oven to 375°F.

In a large Dutch oven over medium-high heat, combine the salt, pasta, and 4 cups of water. Keep covered until boiling. Once boiling, remove the lid and simmer, stirring frequently to make sure pasta isn't sticking and stays submerged. Continue to simmer until most of the liquid has been absorbed, 8 to 10 minutes.

While the pasta is cooking, reheat the ragu in a large saucepan.

When the pasta is al dente and most of the liquid is gone, remove from the heat and, leaving the pasta water, add the ragu to the pasta. Stir thoroughly to combine.

Tear the mozzarella into bite-sized pieces and add it to the pasta. Stir thoroughly to combine.

Bake uncovered for 15 minutes. Sprinkle Parmesan cheese on top and bake an additional 10 to 15 minutes, until the sauce is bubbling, and the cheeses have melted. Allow to rest out of the oven for 10 minutes and then serve.

FETTUCCINI ALFREDO

Yield: 4 servings

¾ cup heavy cream
2 tablespoons unsalted butter
Salt
10 ounces purchased fresh fettuccine pasta
½ cup grated parmesan cheese, plus extra for the table
Ground pepper
Freshly grated nutmeg

In a large sauté pan over medium heat, combine the cream and butter. Bring to a simmer and continue to simmer for a few seconds, stirring until the cream and butter are blended. Remove from the heat and set aside; cover to keep warm.

Bring a large saucepan three-fourths full of water to a rolling boil over high heat. Add 2 tablespoons salt and the fettuccine, stir gently, and quickly bring back to a boil. Boil until al dente, about 2 minutes, then drain well. Add the pasta to the hot cream mixture along with the ½ cup Parmesan, pepper to taste, and a few gratings of nutmeg. Place the sauté pan over high heat. Toss quickly until well blended and hot.

Serve right away on warmed individual plates. Pass additional Parmesan at the table.

Adding vegetables: Broccoli, asparagus, English peas, or sugar snap peas are all great additions to this rich, creamy dish. Add 1 to 2 cups chopped, cooked vegetables to the pasta with the hot cream mixture and toss to coat.

RORY: *"I would never make fun of you. Especially not after you ordered three different kinds of pasta for me just because I couldn't decide."*

DEAN: *"Well you shouldn't have to decide. I mean, tonight, you should have everything that you want."*

RORY: *"I just have to say that I'm now a very big fan of the three-month anniversary."*

PENNE WITH BEEF RAGU

Yield: 4 servings

6 tablespoons olive oil

1 small yellow onion, finely chopped

3 large cloves garlic, minced

1 carrot, finely chopped

1 celery stalk, finely chopped

1 teaspoon fresh rosemary, minced

¾ pound ground beef

½ cup dry red wine

3 tablespoons tomato paste

2½ cups canned whole plum tomatoes, chopped, with juice

Salt and freshly ground pepper

1 pound penne or orecchiette

To make the sauce, in a large, deep frying pan or Dutch oven over medium-low heat, warm the olive oil. Add the onion, garlic, carrot, celery, and rosemary and sauté until the vegetables are softened, about 8 minutes. Add 1 to 2 tablespoons water if necessary to keep the pan from drying out and the vegetables from browning. Add the meat and cook, breaking it up with a wooden spoon, until it is browned, about 10 minutes. Add the wine and the tomato paste. Cook, stirring occasionally, until most of the alcohol has evaporated, about 4 minutes. Reduce the heat to low and add the tomatoes, 1 teaspoon salt, and ½ teaspoon pepper. Cover partially and cook, stirring occasionally, until the sauce is thick and aromatic, about 1 hour.

Meanwhile, cook the pasta. Bring a large pot of water to a boil. Add 2 tablespoons salt and the pasta. Cook, stirring occasionally to prevent sticking, until al dente, according to the package directions. Drain and add to the sauce, stirring to combine. Warm briefly over low heat to blend the flavors. Season to taste with salt and pepper and serve.

TIP: Ragù—which can be made with ground beef, pork, veal, or a combination—tastes even better the day after it is made. This recipe can easily be doubled and will keep in an airtight container for up to 3 days in the refrigerator or for up to 3 months in the freezer.

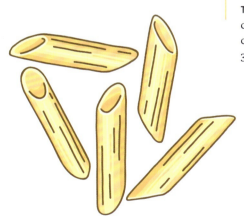

CASHEW
Chicken

When Rory decided to come out at the debutante ball, Lorelai gave her a crash course on being a lady. Ladies don't get their own egg rolls. Ladies never kid. Ladies need help with everything. And a *great* lady can spit the nuts from their chicken right back into the Chinese food container without anyone noticing. This Cashew Chicken marinates in a gingery soy sauce and tastes just as good as Al's.

YIELD: 4 servings

3 tablespoons soy sauce, divided

1 tablespoon rice wine or dry sherry

2 teaspoons grated ginger

1 pound skinless, boneless chicken thighs, cut into bite-sized pieces

1 teaspoon Worcestershire sauce

1 teaspoon Asian sesame oil

½ teaspoon granulated sugar

¼ teaspoon cornstarch (corn flour)

3 tablespoons corn or peanut oil, divided

2 green (spring) onions, chopped

1 cup salted roasted cashews

Steamed rice, for serving

To marinate the chicken, in a large bowl, stir together 2 tablespoons of the soy sauce, the wine, and the ginger. Add in the chicken, coat evenly, and set aside for 15 minutes.

To make the sauce, in a small bowl, combine 2 tablespoons water, the remaining 1 tablespoon soy sauce, and the Worcestershire sauce, sesame oil, sugar, and cornstarch and stir to dissolve the sugar and cornstarch.

To stir-fry the chicken, heat a wok or large frying pan over high heat until very hot and add 2 tablespoons of the corn oil. Remove the chicken from the marinade, draining it well, and discard the marinade. Add the chicken to the wok and stir-fry until white, about 3 minutes. Using a slotted spoon, transfer the chicken to a bowl. Return the pan to medium heat and add the remaining 1 tablespoon corn oil. Add the green onions and stir-fry for about 10 seconds until fragrant. Return the chicken to the pan and add the cashews. Give the sauce a quick stir, add to the pan, and cook-stir until the sauce thickens slightly, 1 to 2 minutes. Serve with the rice.

PARIS: *"No men. Just lots and lots of Chinese food."*

RORY: *"I'll eat to that."*

VEGETABLE
Chow Mein

Looking for the best Chinese food in Stars Hollow? Look no further than Al's Pancake World! Al got bored soon after opening his pancake house and now offers a variety of international cuisines, depending on his mood. His chow mein sandwich has gotten some good buzz, so here's a delicious vegetarian recipe to indulge in. (It's your call if you want to put it in sandwich form.)

YIELD: 4 servings

½ pound fresh Chinese egg noodles

5 tablespoons corn or peanut oil, divided

2 tablespoons oyster sauce

2 tablespoons soy sauce

2 tablespoons rice vinegar

1 tablespoon Asian sesame oil

1 teaspoon granulated sugar (optional)

½ yellow onion, thinly sliced

1 red bell pepper, seeded and thinly sliced lengthwise

¼ pound shiitake mushrooms, stems discarded and caps thinly sliced

1 zucchini, trimmed and cut into matchsticks

1 tablespoon grated ginger

2 cloves garlic, minced

First, parboil the noodles and make the sauce. Bring a large pot of water to a boil. Add the noodles, boil for 2 minutes, drain into a colander, and rinse well with cold running water. Place in a bowl, add 1 tablespoon of the corn oil, and toss to coat evenly. In a small bowl, stir together 3 tablespoons water and the oyster sauce, soy sauce, vinegar, sesame oil, and sugar and stir to dissolve the sugar.

To stir-fry the vegetables, heat a wok or large frying pan over high heat until very hot and add 2 tablespoons of the corn oil. Add the onion and bell pepper and stir-fry just until tender, about 2 minutes. Add the mushrooms and zucchini and continue to stir-fry until golden brown, about 2 minutes. Using a slotted spoon, transfer the vegetables to a bowl.

To stir-fry the noodles, return the pan to high heat and add the remaining 2 tablespoons corn oil. Add the ginger and garlic and stir-fry for about 5 seconds until fragrant. Add the noodles and cook until heated through, about 5 minutes. Return the vegetables to the pan, add the sauce, and continue to stir and toss until all the ingredients are well combined and heated through, about 1 minute. Transfer to a platter and serve.

TIP: You may add meat, poultry, or seafood to this dish, such as ½ pound pork loin; skinless, boneless chicken thighs, cut into thin strips; or peeled shrimp (prawns), chopped. Add to the pan after stir-frying the ginger and garlic and cook just until cooked through, 3 to 4 minutes. Then proceed as directed.

"People don't realize it, but it takes years of training to eat the way we do."

LORELAI

RED VELVET
Cake

It was no surprise when the bristly Michel bristled at Luke dropping by the Dragonfly Inn to handle some odd jobs. What *was* surprising was when the bristly Michel dropped his facade and let Lorelai know how much their monthly afternoon meetings at Weston's, (drinking very large coffees and splitting a slice of red velvet cake and gossiping—and actually he eats the whole cake) mean to him. What's sweeter: this moist, spongey cake with a cream cheese frosting or Michel's saccharine confession that "people come to work for more than just the money?"

YIELD: One 8-inch layer cake

FOR THE CAKE:

½ cup unsalted butter, at room temperature, plus more for greasing

2½ cups all-purpose flour, plus more for dusting

¼ cup unsweetened cocoa powder

1 teaspoon baking powder

1 teaspoon kosher salt

1½ cups buttermilk

2 tablespoons red food coloring

2 cups sugar

2 large eggs

2 teaspoons pure vanilla extract

1½ teaspoons baking soda

1 tablespoon distilled white vinegar

FOR THE FROSTING:

1 cup unsalted butter, at room temperature

3 cups powdered sugar

½ teaspoon kosher salt

1 teaspoon pure vanilla extract

1 pound cold cream cheese

2 tablespoons heavy cream

To make the cake, preheat the oven to 350°F. Grease two 8-inch round cake pans, line the bottoms of the pans with parchment paper, and then grease the parchment. Dust with flour, then tap out any excess.

In a bowl, sift together the flour, cocoa powder, baking powder, and salt. In a small bowl, whisk together the buttermilk and food coloring. Set aside.

In the bowl of a stand mixer fitted with the paddle attachment, beat together the butter and sugar on medium speed until light and fluffy, about 2 minutes. Add the eggs one at a time and then the vanilla and beat until incorporated, about 1 minute. Reduce the speed to low and add the flour mixture in 3 additions, alternating with the buttermilk and beginning and ending with the flour, and beat until combined. In a small bowl, whisk together the baking soda and vinegar. When the fizzing subsides, use a rubber spatula to fold it into the batter.

Divide the batter evenly between the prepared pans. Bake until a toothpick inserted into the center of the cakes comes out clean, 35 to 40 minutes. Transfer the pans to wire racks and let cool for 10 minutes, then invert the cakes onto the racks and let cool completely.

To make the cream cheese frosting, in the bowl of a stand mixer fitted with the paddle attachment, beat the butter on medium speed until smooth, about 1 minute. Reduce the speed to low, add the powdered sugar, and beat until combined, stopping the mixer to scrape down the sides of the bowl as needed. Add the salt and vanilla and raise the speed to medium-high. Add the cream cheese about 1 tablespoon at a time until combined and no bits of cream cheese remain, about 2 minutes. Raise the speed to high, add the cream, and beat until combined, 30 to 45 seconds.

To assemble the cake, place one cake layer on a serving plate. Spread about one-third of the frosting onto the top of the cake and spread evenly with an offset spatula. Place the other layer on top. Cover the entire cake with a thin layer of frosting and refrigerate for 30 minutes. Working with the chilled cake, spread the remaining cream cheese frosting on the top and sides of the cake.

YE OLDE
Butter Brickle Crunch Ice Cream

Taylor may have railroaded his way into the store next to Luke's but there's no denying that his Olde Fashioned Soda Shoppe is the perfect addition to whimsical downtown Stars Hollow—not to mention, he serves all the Gilmore Girls' favorite foods: milkshakes, hot chocolate, candy, and ice cream. This Butter Brickle Crunch Ice Cream will have you tugging on a poodle skirt and asking your beau to the sock hop. Enjoy the ice cream's salty-sweet toffee swirl and crunchy toffee chips on its own or add cream soda for a float.

YIELD: About 6 cups

2 cups toffee chips, divided

2 cups plus 2 tablespoons heavy whipping cream, divided

1½ teaspoons vanilla paste

One 14-ounce can sweetened condensed milk

Chilled cream soda, optional

In a small saucepan, combine 1 cup of the toffee chips with 2 tablespoons of the heavy whipping cream. Over medium-low heat, stir to combine and continue cooking until melted, stirring frequently. Note: If your toffee chips contain nuts, your mixture will not be completely smooth, and that's okay. Remove from heat and allow to cool while making the ice cream.

In the bowl of a stand mixer, whip the cream on high until stiff peaks form. Stir in the vanilla and then gently fold in the sweetened condensed milk until no streaks remain. Add the melted toffee chips and stir until combined. Add the remaining toffee chips and stir to combine.

Transfer to a shallow, airtight container, and freeze for a minimum of 6 hours but preferably overnight. Stirring the mixture after about 3 to 4 hours of freezing will help create an even distribution of toffee swirl and toffee chips.

This ice cream base can be adjusted easily to other flavors. Leave out the toffee chips and fold in small chunks of Homemade Edible Cookie Dough (page 109), chocolate chips, or your favorite crushed cookie!

To create a float, place two scoops of ice cream in a tall soda glass and fill with cream soda.

"Oh, well, gosh, look at all the choices, really hard to pick. I think I'll try a scoop of butter brickle crunch."

LORELAI

LORELAI'S
Giant Birthday Pizza

Rory wants to ring in Lorelai's 35th birthday with the WORLD'S BIGGEST PIZZA, but as it turns out the WORLD'S BIGGEST PIZZA is roughly half the size of a football field, and Antolioni can't accommodate that. But Rory still manages to pull off a pretty big pizza, big enough at least to leave Kirk badly maimed. Here's a modified recipe for a giant pizza that doesn't require the WORLD'S BIGGEST OVEN. Be careful when sliding your pizza in and out of the oven so you don't end up like Kirk!

YIELD: 3 giant pizzas

FOR THE DOUGH
4½ teaspoons active dry yeast
2¼ teaspoons sugar
2¼ cups lukewarm water (about 115°F)
4½ cups bread flour
1 tablespoon kosher salt
2 tablespoons olive oil

FOR THE TOMATO SAUCE
2 tablespoons olive oil
2 cloves garlic, minced
½ cup dry white wine
1 bay leaf
One 28-ounce can crushed tomatoes
1 tablespoon tomato paste
2 teaspoons sugar
1 teaspoon dried oregano
Kosher salt and freshly ground pepper
½ cup fresh basil leaves, finely chopped (optional)

FOR THE TOPPINGS
2 pounds shredded mozzarella
3 ounces of pepperoni, optional
1 pound ground Italian sausage, browned and drained, optional
1 small yellow onion, diced, optional

To make the dough, in the bowl of a stand mixer, stir together the yeast, sugar, and water. Let stand until bubbles form on top, about 5 minutes. Fit the mixer with the paddle attachment. Add the flour and salt and beat on low speed until combined. Switch to the dough hook. Slowly drizzle in the oil and knead until the dough comes together into a ball and pulls away from the sides of the bowl, about 5 minutes. Remove the bowl from the mixer and cover the bowl with plastic wrap. Let rise at room temperature until the dough is doubled in size, about 1 hour.

To make the sauce, in a large sauté pan over medium heat, warm the oil. Add the garlic and cook, stirring occasionally, until fragrant, about 1 minute. Add the wine and bay leaf and bring to a simmer, then cook, stirring occasionally, until reduced by half, about 5 minutes. Add the tomatoes, tomato paste, sugar, oregano, and a pinch each of salt and pepper. Simmer, stirring occasionally, until the sauce thickens, and the flavors deepen, about 20 minutes. Remove from the heat and adjust the seasoning with salt and pepper. Remove and discard the bay leaf. Stir in the basil, if using. Let cool. Use right away or transfer to an airtight container and refrigerate for up to 1 week.

Have 3 large cookie sheets covered in parchment standing by. Split the dough into thirds, working with 1 piece at a time, stretch the dough into the shape of a giant pizza slice. Make sure to use the whole piece of parchment to maximize the size of your slice. As you stretch the dough, make sure to leave the edges slightly thicker, especially at the top, widest part, of the slice, finish with a nice point. Continue with the remaining pieces of dough. Let the "slices" rest for 20 minutes before topping. While the pizzas are resting, preheat the oven to 450°F.

Cover each pizza with about a ⅓ cup of sauce and ⅓ of the cheese, leaving the top crust clear but getting as close to the edges as possible. Finish with the other toppings. Either let your guests choose or make sure you have something for everyone!

Bake 1 giant slice at a time by sliding the parchment directly on the lowest oven rack, bake for 15 to 18 minutes or until the crust is crisp and golden brown and the cheese is melted and bubbling. Use the cookie sheet to remove pizza from the oven by sliding the parchment back on to it.

STEAK &
SIX BAKED POTATOES
For Four People

Max's shellshock at his first night in Stars Hollow prompted good guy Dean to sit him down and give him a quick and dirty rundown of life with the Gilmore Girls: the danger in using the last of the Parmesan cheese, how to improv with Lorelai using a pepperoni and a mushroom, their affinity for puppies, and, of course, their unmatched eating habits. Come on, Max, if six baked potatoes for four people surprises you, that's a huge red flag.

STEAK

YIELD: 4 to 6 servings

Two 1½-pound, bone-in New York strip, porterhouse, or T-bone steaks

1 teaspoon salt

Fresh ground black pepper, to taste

4 tablespoons butter, softened

1 packed tablespoon thyme leaves, stemmed and chopped

Pinch of red pepper flakes

1 tablespoon canola oil

Shishito peppers (or red bell peppers, thinly sliced), optional

A half hour before cooking, rub both sides of the steaks with the salt and pepper and set aside to rest.

Make a compound butter by combining the butter, thyme, and red pepper flakes in a small bowl. Set aside.

Heat the oil in a large cast iron or stainless-steel skillet on medium-high. Just as the oil begins to shimmer, carefully place the steaks into the skillet. Brown for 4 minutes on each side, or until a deep brown crust has formed. Do not disturb during the 4 minutes. Add the compound butter to the pan, and carefully use a spoon to baste the steaks with the butter for another 4 to 6 minutes, until the internal temperature reaches 120°F for medium rare or 125°F for medium. Transfer the steaks to a baking sheet, and tent with foil. Let rest for 10 minutes. The steaks will continue to cook during this time.

While the steak is resting, return the pan, with the compound butter, to medium heat and cook the peppers for 5 to 8 minutes, or until soft, stirring occasionally. Allow them to blister in some spots and baste them with the remaining butter in the pan.

If desired, remove the steaks from the bone and slice against the grain. Serve the meat in the pan on top of the peppers.

TIP: A cast-iron or stainless-steel pan works best for this. Do not use a nonstick pan, as they typically aren't meant to handle the heat required.

BAKED POTATOES

YIELD: 4 servings

6 large russet potatoes, scrubbed and dried

3 tablespoons high temperature oil, such as grapeseed or avocado

6 teaspoons kosher salt

½ cup (1 stick) good quality unsalted butter, softened

1 teaspoon dried parsley

1 teaspoon dried chives

Sour cream, for garnish, optional

Fresh ground pepper, for garnish, optional

Green onion, for garnish, optional

Preheat the oven to 375°F.

On a rimmed baking sheet, brush each potato with oil and then rub with a teaspoon of salt.

Bake in the oven for 45 minutes to an hour until fork tender.

While potatoes are baking, combine the butter, parsley, and chives. Blend with a fork. When the mixture is well blended, turn out onto a piece of parchment paper and form into a log. Wrap, completely twisting the ends to close and refrigerate.

When the potatoes are ready, split them end to end with a sharp knife and add a few slices of the compound butter. Top with sour cream, fresh ground pepper, and green onion, if using.

MAX: *"How can they possibly eat more?"*

DEAN: *"Kind of surprised."*

MAX: *"I know. They're bottomless pits."*

DEAN: *"I mean at you. You've known them long enough not to be so confused."*

BEEF
Noodle Salad

Some of Stars Hollow's best Asian cuisine comes from the Pancake House, and you'd be lucky to pull this meal on International Grab Bag Night at Al's. This Vietnamese noodle dish has marinated sirloin or flank steak, noodles dressed with a limey dressing, and fresh herbs and spices.

YIELD: 4 servings

6 cloves garlic, minced

½ cup unsweetened coconut milk

½ cup Asian fish sauce, divided

2 tablespoons plus 1½ teaspoons light brown sugar, firmly packed

One 1-pound sirloin or flank steak, about 1½ inches thick

6 ounces dried rice vermicelli or rice stick noodles, soaked in hot water for 15 minutes and drained

Juice from 2 limes

6 tablespoons corn or peanut oil, divided

3 shallots, thinly sliced

½ cup thinly sliced cucumber, Persian or English preferred

1 red or green jalapeno chile, seeded and thinly sliced

½ cup fresh Thai basil, slivered

¼ cup fresh mint, slivered

To marinate the steak and prepare the grill, in a shallow dish, combine half the garlic, the coconut milk, ¼ cup of the fish sauce, and 2 tablespoons brown sugar and stir to dissolve the sugar. Add the steak, turn to coat, cover, and let stand for 20 minutes. Prepare a gas or charcoal grill for direct grilling over high heat.

Meanwhile, make the salad. Bring a large pot of water to a boil. Plunge the vermicelli into the water and boil for just 5 seconds. Drain immediately but do not rinse, and place in a large bowl. In a blender, combine the remaining garlic, the remaining ¼ cup fish sauce, the remaining 1½ teaspoons brown sugar, the lime juice, and 5 tablespoons of the oil. Process until smooth to make the dressing. Scatter the shallots, cucumber, chile, basil, and mint over the noodles, drizzle with the dressing, and toss to mix well. Set aside.

To grill the beef, remove the steak from the marinade, discard the marinade, and pat the steak dry. Lightly oil the grill rack with the remaining tablespoon of oil, and place the steak on the grill. Cook, turning once, until well browned on both sides and medium-rare at the center, 4 to 5 minutes on each side. Transfer to a cutting board and let rest for 2 minutes. Thinly slice across the grain, capturing any juices. Arrange the slices on top of the salad, drizzle with the juices, and serve.

TIP: To save time, grill the steak in a stove-top grill pan. Preheat over high heat, brush with oil, and use the same timing.

LORELAI: *"We are so in luck. It was international grab bag night at Al's."*

RORY: *"Cool. Did you peek?"*

LORELAI: *"And ruin the whole point of the mystery dinner? I think not."*

SHRIMP
From Al's Pancake World

Al's shrimp gets a bad rap because it sometimes makes people sick to their stomachs, and possibly because Lorelai tried to use it to fake food poisoning so she and Luke could dip out of dinner with her parents early. But the only reason this shrimp will leave your stomach hurting is because it's seasoned with plenty of cayenne pepper and so spicy and scrumptious you won't be able to stop eating it.

YIELD: 2 to 4 servings

1 pound jumbo or large shrimp

1 tablespoon minced garlic

1 teaspoon kosher salt

1 tablespoon grated fresh ginger

1½ to 2 teaspoons cayenne pepper

1 teaspoon freshly ground black pepper

1 teaspoon ground cumin

½ teaspoon ground cinnamon

¼ teaspoon ground cloves

¼ teaspoon ground turmeric

2 tablespoons gin

1 teaspoon dark brown sugar, firmly packed

2 tablespoons mustard oil or olive oil

1 tablespoon fresh lemon juice

Chopped fresh cilantro (optional)

Peel the shrimp, with the tail segments intact, and then devein them and place in a shallow dish. In a small bowl, combine the garlic, salt, ginger, cayenne, black pepper, cumin, cinnamon, cloves, turmeric, gin, and brown sugar and mix well to form a paste. Rub the paste evenly over the shrimp. Let sit at room temperature for about 30 minutes.

In a large frying pan, warm the oil over high heat. When the oil is very hot, add the shrimp and cook, tossing, until they turn pink and opaque, about 5 minutes.

Remove from the heat, sprinkle with the lemon juice and cilantro, if using, transfer to a serving dish, and serve.

"You ate shrimp at a pancake house? Well, of course your stomach's unsettled."

EMILY

LORELAI: "Hey, let's look into each other's eyes and say 'I wish I were you' at exactly the same time. Maybe we'll pull a 'Freaky Friday'."

RORY: "Or we can just pretend like we did, and you can go around acting really immature. Oh, wait..."

FOUNDER'S DAY
Punch

The $3 admission to the Stars Hollow Museum includes a cup of Miss Patty's Founder's Day punch—and boy does it punch. This drink is fruity and fizzy, and it can be warmed up and spiced for a cold weather version. Add 750 milliliters of spiced rum if you want to turn it into a cocktail but remember that version is safest to consume on a full stomach and an unbroken heart. *(DISCLAIMER: Miss Patty is not responsible for hangovers or drunk dials to ex-boyfriends.)*

YIELD: 12 servings

32 ounces unsweetened cranberry juice

48 ounces unfiltered apple cider

6 ounces pineapple juice

24 ounces ginger beer

2 whole cinnamon sticks, for cold weather variation

750 milliliters spiced rum, optional

In a large pitcher or drink dispenser, combine the cranberry, apple, and pineapple juices. Refrigerate for at least 4 hours or until ready to serve.

Just before serving, add ginger beer and stir gently. Pour over glasses filled with ice.

If using the rum, add it to the drink dispenser with the juices or add about 2 ounces to each 8-ounce glass.

For a cold weather version, in a large pot add the cranberry, apple, and pineapple juices and the cinnamon sticks. Bring to a low boil over medium heat and then remove from the heat. Add the ginger beer and serve in mugs. Spike with rum, if desired.

RORY: *"Miss Patty's leftover punch is used to remove tar from construction sites."*

PARIS: *"Then let it remove the tar from our souls."*

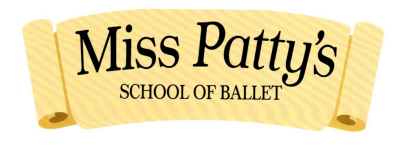

Miss Patty's
SCHOOL OF BALLET

Founder's PUNCH

Lorelai and Rory's House

When Digger Stiles sets Richard up on wireless internet, Richard asks Lorelai if she and Rory have gone wireless. "Oh, no," she replies, "we're pretty wired most of the time."

Wired is one understated way to describe the quick wit, speedy convos, and admirable work ethic of this mother/daughter duo. Needless to say, there's a lot of caffeine and a lot of sugar in Lorelai and Rory's house. How else are they going to fuel 100-mile-a-minute chatter? But don't worry, if you're trying to limit processed sugars in your diet, there's a salad, if you're into that kind of thing.

MOVIE NIGHT
Snack Board

Whether you're catching a showing of *Willy Wonka and the Chocolate Factory* or staying in to watch *Tears and Laughter: The Joan and Melissa Rivers Story* in your pajamas, what's the point of movie night if you don't have the right snacks? This snack board includes four flavored popcorns and Homemade Peanut Butter Sandwich Cookies (page 106), and Lorelai likes to add carrot sticks to make sure Rory is eating right. Recreate this board exactly or personalize it with all your favorite candies.

YIELD: 4 servings

FOR THE POPCORNS

FLAVOR ONE

12 cups air popped or plain microwave popcorn

2 tablespoons of ghee, melted

¼ cup shelf-stable Parmesan cheese

½ teaspoon garlic powder

FLAVOR TWO

12 cups air popped or plain microwave popcorn

2 tablespoons of ghee, melted

2 tablespoons of Cheddar cheese powder

FLAVOR THREE

12 cups air popped or plain microwave popcorn

2 tablespoons of ghee, melted

2 packs of powdered candy dip

FLAVOR FOUR

12 cups air popped or plain microwave popcorn

2 tablespoons of ghee, melted

¼ cup sugar

1 teaspoon cinnamon

A selection of candies such as red licorice sticks, marshmallows, jelly beans, chocolate kisses, and whatever else your heart desires

Homemade Peanut Butter Sandwich Cookies (page 106)

Carrot sticks

Chips

Beverages of choice

In a large bowl, toss the popcorn with the melted ghee, making sure to thoroughly coat it. Add the spices for whichever flavor you're creating, if using, or the cheese and toss again to coat. Serve immediately.

To set up for movie night: Place popcorn in a large serving bowl with paper popcorn holders or smaller bowls for individual servings. On a large cutting board or serving tray, arrange the candies, cookies, and carrot sticks in small bowls or glasses for easy grabbing. Don't be afraid to use vertical space. Have small paper bags or cups nearby so guests can create their own custom mix and avoid sharing!

DEAN: *"So at what point does an outsider get to suggest a movie for movie night?"*

RORY: *"That depends. What movie are you thinking of?"*

DEAN: *"I don't know . . . Boogie Nights maybe?"*

RORY: *"You'll never get it past Lorelai."*

HOMEMADE
Peanut Butter Sandwich Cookies

Who invented the peanut butter sandwich cookie? Some genius, that's who. These cookies, a staple in the Gilmore household for any number of occasions, are just the right amount of sweet, just the right amount of salty, just the right amount of peanut buttery, and just the right amount of shaped-like-a-peanut. Make your own sandwich cookies and smooth peanut butter filling with this recipe. So cute, so genius.

YIELD: About 24 sandwich cookies

FOR THE COOKIES
10 tablespoons butter,
at room temperature
½ cup smooth peanut butter
½ cup brown sugar, firmly packed
1 egg
2 cups all-purpose flour

FOR THE FILLING
½ cup smooth peanut butter
2 tablespoons powdered sugar

RORY: *"Hello."*

LORELAI: *"Did you bring the Nutter Butters?"*

RORY: *"Well, I'm fine, Mother. I missed you, too."*

LORELAI: *"Ah, we have achieved culinary perfection."*

Preheat oven to 350°F. Line two cookie sheets with silicone baking mats or parchment paper.

To make the cookies, in the bowl of a stand mixer, combine the butter, peanut butter, brown sugar, and egg. Beat until smooth.

Add the flour and beat until the dough comes together and pulls away from the side of the bowl.

To create the classic peanut shape, roll dough into 1-inch balls and then shape into logs, about 2 inches long. Place on prepared cookie sheets, leaving 2 inches of space in between each cookie.

Use a fork to mark the log long ways, pressing down to flatten. Then use the fork in the other direction to further flatten and create the cross hatch.

Bake 10 to 12 minutes or until crisp and starting to brown at the edges. Allow to cool completely.

To create the filling, use a fork to thoroughly blend the peanut butter and powdered sugar together in a small bowl.

Place a dollop of frosting at each end of one peanut cookie, top with another cookie, and press down gently.

TIP: Speed up your experience by rolling the balls slightly bigger and using your thumb to create an indent. Bake for 8 minutes and then fill with peanut butter filling before baking another 2 to 4 minutes. Alternatively, during the second bake, the thumb prints can be filled with strawberry or raspberry jam for a peanut butter and jelly cookie.

HOMEMADE
Edible Cookie Dough

Cookie dough is the ultimate comfort food, be it cooked or uncooked. Tough day at work? Cookie dough. Studying for finals? Cookie dough. Movie night? Cookie dough. Devastated from a tough break up with your fiancé after hooking up with your high school sweetheart and father of your child? So relatable! Have some cookie dough. This recipe is safe to consume raw. Eat it plain, frozen, and dipped in chocolate or fold it into homemade ice cream before freezing.

YIELD: About 3 cups

1 cup rolled oats
½ cup white rice flour
2 teaspoons vanilla extract
½ teaspoon salt
2 tablespoons milk of choice
½ cup butter, room temperature
¼ cup granulated sugar
½ cup light brown sugar, packed
1 cup chocolate chips
10 ounces dark chocolate melting wafers, optional

In the bowl of a food processor, pulse the rolled oats and rice flour together until combined. With the processor running, continue to work oats and rice flour until it is the consistency of cornmeal, about 2 to 3 minutes.

Add in the vanilla, salt, and milk. Pulse several times until combined. Add the sugars and pulse again until combined.

Cut the butter into small pieces, add to the food processor, and run until the dough comes together, about 1 minute.

Transfer to a medium bowl and stir in chocolate chips.

Store in an airtight container or form into logs and wrap in parchment paper. Refrigerate until serving.

The cookie dough can be scooped into 1-inch balls, chilled, and dipped in chocolate. Prepare a cookie sheet with parchment paper, place the cookie dough balls on the sheet, and chill for 20 minutes. Melt the chocolate in a microwave safe bowl, 30 seconds at time, stirring as you go. Using a fork to hold each ball, dip in chocolate until completely covered, allow excess chocolate to drip off, and place on the parchment covered cookie sheet. Allow to set for 15 to 20 minutes. Serve immediately or store in an airtight container in the refrigerator.

LUKE: *"There's nothing in here but ice cream, candy bars, cookie dough, and canned frosting. Why are you not four hundred and fifty pounds?"*

LORELAI: *"I know. Scientists call it the Lorelai paradox."*

RORY'S PRETZELS
From
Around The World

Rory and Naked Marty's Marx Brothers movie night ends on a rough note, but at least these pretzels offer a tasty twist. Rory's Pretzels from Around the World is an international spread showcasing churro-inspired cinnamon pretzels, Swiss chocolate-covered pretzels, and super-hot wasabi nuggets that'll have your mouth numb in under a minute.

YIELD: 12 soft pretzels

FOR THE SOFT PRETZEL DOUGH
1 cup warm water (110°F)

2¼ teaspoons (1 package) active dry yeast

1 tablespoon sugar

6 tablespoons unsalted butter, melted, divided

3¼ cups all-purpose flour, plus more for dusting

1 teaspoon kosher salt

Vegetable oil, for brushing

½ tablespoon cocoa powder

1 tablespoon cinnamon sugar, divided

1 teaspoon wasabi powder, divided

1/3 cup baking soda

½ cup brown sugar

Coarse salt, for sprinkling

FOR THE WASABI MUSTARD
¼ cup yellow mustard

½ teaspoon wasabi powder

FOR THE GANACHE
4 ounces milk chocolate chips

2 tablespoons of heavy cream

To make the dough, in the bowl of a stand mixer, stir together the warm water, yeast, and sugar. Let stand until foamy, about 10 minutes. Add 3 tablespoons of the butter, flour, and salt. Attach the dough hook and knead the dough on medium-low speed until smooth, about 10 minutes. Form the dough into a ball, cover the bowl with plastic wrap, and let rise in a warm spot until doubled in size, about 1 hour.

Line two baking sheets with parchment paper and brush the parchment with vegetable oil. Dump the dough onto a lightly floured work surface, cut into three equal pieces, and work with one piece at a time. Keep the remaining dough covered with a damp kitchen towel to prevent it from drying out.

For the Swiss chocolate pretzels, work ½ tablespoon cocoa powder into the dough, letting it be marbled. Split into 4 equal pieces and roll each into an 18-inch rope. With each rope positioned horizontally, bring the ends up and toward the center as if forming an oval; cross one end over the other, and press each end into the bottom of the oval to create a pretzel shape. Place the pretzels on the prepared baking sheets, spacing them evenly.

For the cinnamon sugar pretzels, work ½ tablespoon of cinnamon sugar into the dough, again letting it be marbled, and divide it into 4 equal pieces. Create the ropes but cut each rope in half and create 8 mini pretzels. Place on the prepared baking sheet.

For the wasabi pretzel bites, take the last piece of dough and work ½ teaspoon of wasabi powder into the dough. Divide the dough into 4 equal pieces and create thick 6-inch ropes. Cut each rope into thirds. Mix another ½ teaspoon wasabi powder with coarse salt and set aside.

Position a rack in the middle of the oven and preheat to 450°F. Fill a large, wide saucepan with 7 cups water, stir in the baking soda and brown sugar, and bring to a boil over high heat.

Working with the chocolate pretzels first and ending with the wasabi bites, gently drop 2 or 3 pretzels at a time into the boiling water (be careful not to overcrowd them). Boil for just under 1 minute, turning once with a large slotted spoon or spider. Return the boiled pretzels to the baking sheets, top side up. Bake for 5 minutes and then brush with melted butter and sprinkle the cinnamon pretzels with more cinnamon sugar and the wasabi bites with the wasabi salt.

Bake for an additional 5 minutes or until golden brown. Serve warm. Serve Swiss chocolate pretzels with milk chocolate ganache and the wasabi pretzels with wasabi mustard.

To make the wasabi mustard, combine the mustard and ½ teaspoon of wasabi powder and let stand for 5 minutes.

To make the ganache, in a microwave-safe bowl, cover the chocolate chips with the cream and microwave for 45 seconds. Let stand for 5 minutes and then stir until smooth. If the chocolate does not melt all the way, microwave for 10 seconds more.

RORY: *"Pretzels of the world. San Francisco sourdough. German pumpernickel, chocolate-covered Swiss, and the wasabi bites are very intriguing. I also ordered a pizza before you got here."*

MARTY: *"Okay, well at least we got the food part covered."*

LIME FANTASY SUPREME

With Two Spoons

Honey, I'm home! Don't make the same mistake Dean did and imply that a Gilmore Girl's place is in the kitchen . . . unless it's to dig a carton of ice cream out from the back of the freezer. But, if you ever feel like embracing your inner Donna Reed, throw on some heels and a string of pearls and labor over this lime and whipped cream dessert. Serve with two spoons so you and your honey can gaze lovingly at each other while you share a dessert and remind him that Donna directed and produced her own show and was an all-around total boss.

YIELD: 4 servings

1½ cups boiling water

One 6-ounce box of lime gelatin

2 unflavored gelatin packets (about 5 teaspoons)

1 cup cold water filled with ice to make 2½ cups ice water

One 11-ounce can mandarin orange segments, drained and juice reserved

½ cup heavy whipping cream

2 tablespoons sugar

In a large heatproof bowl, combine the boiling water, lime gelatin, and unflavored gelatin and stir until gelatin is dissolved. Add the ice water and stir together until all the ice is melted and the mixture is slightly thickened.

Pour the gelatin into an 8-by-8-inch baking pan. Place segments of mandarin oranges in neat rows, leaving about an inch in between, across the baking pan. Each one will be the center of a gelatin cube. Press down slightly until the mandarin segments are underneath the gelatin's surface. Refrigerate for at least 6 hours.

Just before serving, combine the whipping cream, 2 tablespoons mandarin juice, and sugar. Whip until soft peaks form.

To serve, cut the gelatin into cubes keeping mandarin slices whole. Fill a glass with cubes and top with a large dollop of whipped cream. Serve immediately or refrigerate.

"I must now sublimate all my impure thoughts by going into the kitchen and making an endless string of perfect casseroles."

RORY

DESSERT
Sushi

When Logan jets off to London to start his new job, he and Rory have to cancel their trip to Asia, so Lorelai, in true Lorelai fashion, brings Asia to Stars Hollow. Building an *exact replica* of Asia in their living room, she and Rory visit Japan, China, Vietnam, Cambodia, and Korea. No tour of Asia is complete without totally authentic Asian cuisine, like this dessert sushi made with cookies, "wasabi" frosting, and tons of candy.

YIELD: About 30 pieces

1 package chocolate sandwich cookies
Green food coloring
6 cups puffed rice cereal
4 cups mini marshmallows
3 tablespoons butter
4 to 6 dark colored fruit leathers
Plenty of candy, such as gummy fish or sour belts
Marshmallow fluff, optional, as "glue"

Line a rimmed baking sheet with parchment paper. Separate the sandwich cookie halves. Keep 6 to 8 halves with frosting to create a sushi bite.

Scrape frosting off remaining sandwich halves into a bowl and combine with green food coloring to create "wasabi" glue. Set aside.

In the bowl of a food processor, pulverize the non-frosted cookie halves to a fine crumb and set aside.

Have the puffed rice cereal standing by in a large bowl. In a microwave-safe bowl, add the marshmallows and the butter, microwave for 1 minute, and stir until smooth.

Pour the marshmallow mixture into the rice cereal and stir, making sure all the cereal is coated and sticking together.

Spread the puffed rice cereal thinly, between ¼ and ½ inch thick, onto the prepared baking sheet. Trim square and reserve the scraps to create nigiri style sushi pieces. Use "wasabi" frosting or marshmallow fluff to glue strips of fruit leather together as nori.

Cut the rice cereal sheet into quarters, about 3 inches wide. Create sushi rolls by spreading a thin strip of "wasabi" frosting onto the center of a rice treat rectangle topped with various candies. Roll into a log and compress gently to keep together. Roll the log into the cookie crumbs, covering completely, and slice.

Get creative! Just like a sushi party you can set up all the ingredients and let guests build their own.

LORELAI: *"I am telling you the invention of dessert sushi is gonna make us our first million."*

RORY: *"And our second."*

LORELAI: *"I'd like our third to be go-go dancing."*

CREAM PUFFS
For Hands

Lorelai's had some pretty weird dreams, like the one where she takes (real) Paul Anka out for a walk and (dog) Paul Anka runs into the street, and it ends with (real) Paul Anka sitting in Babette's lap, or the one where she steps into a boxing ring only to find she has cream puffs for hands. These cream puffs are so decadent, it's unreal. If you need a totem to ground yourself in reality, check your hands: if they're cream puffs, you're probably dreaming.

YIELD: 6 boxing glove cream puffs

FOR THE PÂTE À CHOUX
1 cup whole milk

½ cup unsalted butter, cut into chunks about the size of a tablespoon

1 tablespoon sugar

½ teaspoon salt

1 cup of all-purpose flour

4 eggs, at room temperature

FOR THE CREAM FILLING
1 cup heavy whipping cream

1 teaspoon vanilla

1 tablespoon instant coffee

2 tablespoons powdered sugar, plus additional for dusting

Line two cookie sheets with a silicone mat or parchment paper. Preheat the oven to 400°F.

In a large saucepan over medium-high heat, combine the milk, butter, sugar, and salt.

Bring to a boil and add the flour all at once. Stir vigorously with a wooden spoon until the mixture is smooth and is not sticking to the spoon or the pot. If the mixture looks rough or butter leaks out, just keep stirring until it comes together. When the mixture is smooth and formed into dough, remove it from the heat and transfer it to a bowl.

Allow the mixture to cool for 5 minutes and then begin adding the eggs one at a time. Beat after each egg until it is completely incorporated and the mixture is smooth again.

When all the eggs have been added, place mounded ¼ cup scoops of choux paste onto the prepared cookie sheet, placed 3 inches apart. Dip an offset spatula in water and gently shape the paste into even rounds about 1½ inches high.

Bake for 15 minutes; then turn the oven down to 350°F and bake another 30 to 35 minutes, or until golden brown and firm to the touch.

Remove from the oven and use a skewer or sharp knife to poke holes in a few places around the side of the puff to allow steam to escape. Allow to cool completely.

Once cool, slice the puff in half horizontally and remove any moist uncooked dough.

While the puffs cool, make the filling. In a large bowl, combine the heavy whipping cream, vanilla, and instant coffee. Stir until the coffee is dissolved. Add in the powdered sugar. With a hand mixer on high, whip until stiff peaks form.

TO ASSEMBLE: Fill a pastry bag fitted with a large star tip with the whipped cream and pipe a thick layer of cream on the bottom of each puff. Rest the top piece on the cream and dust with powdered sugar.

NOTE: Puffs and cream can be made a day ahead and stored in separate airtight containers in the refrigerator. Don't assemble until just before serving.

FROZEN PIZZA
With Tater Tots

Frozen food connoisseur Lorelai whips up this incredibly Lorelai-ish snack after coming home starving from a red-wine-reduction dinner with Richard and Emily. Requiring only Lorelai-level cooking skills, this dish calls for a deft turning on of the oven and a careful dumping of warm tater tots on top of a frozen pizza. Always check first to make sure you haven't stored a purse or something in the oven.

YIELD: 4 servings (or 2 Gilmore Girls' servings)

One 28-ounce bag of frozen tater tots

2 regular or thin crust frozen pizzas, preferably cheese or pepperoni

Preheat the oven and cookie sheet 425°F.

When the oven and cookie sheet come up to temperature, bake the tater tots for 20 minutes.

While tater tots are baking, unwrap the pizzas and remove any loose cheese and/or pepperoni from the top of the pizza. Reserve in a bowl.

Remove tater tots from the oven and lower the temperature to 400°F. Cover each pizza with tater tots and sprinkle reserved cheese and pepperoni, if using, on top.

Bake for 15 to 20 minutes or until the crust of pizza is golden.

NOTE: Cooking times may need to be altered according to your pizzas' package directions.

"I love pizza. I eat tons of pizza. It's one of my four major food groups."

LORELAI

COMPLETE
Salad In A Bag

Rumor has it that the vitamin D found in leafy greens is vital to the human body's growth and overall health, but Lorelai and Rory aren't buying it. Until science can prove it, vegetables will not be given preference over burgers and fries. But in a food emergency when you can't get to a pizza, in your most desperate moments when the Chinese takeout is taking too long, salad is, technically, food. Use this creamy ranch to mask the vegetable taste.

Check the bag for serving sizes, although that depends largely on how much you're going to eat and how much you're going to just push around with your fork, and always be sure to wash your bagged greens before consuming.

YIELD: 3 cups of dressing

FOR THE AQUAFABA DRESSING

¾ cup aquafaba (or the reserved chickpea liquid from Mrs. Kim's Eggless Egg Salad Sandwiches on page 75)

½ teaspoon cream of tartar

2 tablespoons Dijon mustard

1 teaspoon garlic powder

2 teaspoons onion powder

½ teaspoon ground black pepper, or to taste

½ teaspoon salt

½ cup neutral oil, such as grapeseed or avocado

¾ olive oil

1 cup loosely packed herbs leaves, such as parsley, chives, thyme, basil, oregano, and rosemary

Bag of salad greens

In a blender, add the aquafaba and the cream of tartar. Blend on low to combine and then continue to blend on high for 2 minutes.

Add the Dijon mustard, garlic powder, onion powder, pepper, and salt, and blend on high for 30 seconds to combine.

In a small bowl, mix the neutral oil and olive oil together.

With the blender running on low, pour in the oils in a steady stream until incorporated. If your blender does not have a spout or hole that you can pour into through the lid, then add a small amount of oil at a time and blend in between additions.

Finely chop the herbs and add them to the blender. Blend to combine.

Decant the dressing to an airtight container and refrigerate until needed. This can be stored for up to 1 week.

Wash a big batch of greens and store in a resealable bag with a damp paper towel so they are ready to go. When ready to eat, open the bag of greens and pour dressing inside. Just make sure to remove the towel before adding the dressing! That's too much ruffage! Enjoy!

"It's a quaint dish sometimes used to precede large quantities of pizza."

DEAN

WALLOWING
Board

Not every day can be sunshine and fizzlesticks. Every once in a while, you run into a problem (ahem: a boy), and you just need a day to wallow. Stay inside in the dark, watch movies, no makeup, don't even *think* about showering, and drown your sorrows in your favorite comfort (ahem: junk) foods. Cookie dough, pizza, tons and tons of ice cream—they're all part of the wallowing process. Don't fight it. Give in to the wallow.

YIELD: 2 servings

1 broken heart and 1 caregiver
Homemade Edible Cookie Dough (page 109)

Ye Olde Butter Brickle Crunch Ice Cream (page 91)

1 pizza with everything (Use Lorelai's Giant Birthday Pizza on page 92 or Frozen Pizza with Tater Tots on page 118 if you are in a wallowing rush!)

1 or 2 boxes of tissues

Large glass of water (You must keep hydrated for a good cry!)

A varied selection of sad movie classics and/or celebrity magazines

Arrange all the food on a tray that can be moved easily from the sofa to your bed as the mood strikes. Keep the spoons handy but leave bowls and plates by the wayside for this event. Place a trash can nearby for discarded tissues and have the remote handy!

"Oh yeah, get back in your pajamas, go to bed, eat nothing but gallons of ice cream and tons of pizza, don't take a shower or shave your legs or put on any kind of make up at all and just sit in the dark and watch a really sad movie and have a good long cry and just wallow. You need to wallow."

LORELAI

NACHOS
& A Slushie

When Taylor started selling trucker food at Doose's to cash in on the trucker crowd coming through Stars Hollow off the highway, he unintentionally stumbled upon the perfect Lorelai snack: nachos and a slushie. The nachos are the star of this show, topped with beans, onions, jalapenos, and a spicy queso. Unlike Taylor, we used real cheese, so it won't turn to rock the moment you stop stirring it.

YIELD: 2 jumbo slushies and 6 to 8 servings of nachos

FOR THE SLUSHIE
1½ cups cherry flavored drink syrup, such as Torani

2 cups cold water

FOR THE NACHO CHEESE
One 12-ounce can evaporated milk

1½ tablespoons cornstarch

3 cups medium Cheddar cheese, shredded

1 teaspoon salt

½ teaspoon garlic powder

¼ teaspoon turmeric

1 teaspoon paprika

½ tablespoon yellow mustard

FOR THE BASE AND TOPPINGS
One 24-ounce bag of corn tortilla chips

Two 15-ounce cans of pinto beans in chili sauce, heated through

1 white onion, diced

One 12-ounce jar of sliced jalapenos

In a 9-by-13-inch glass dish, combine the syrup and water and place in the freezer.

About every 45 minutes, scrape the forming ice particles from the sides of the pan with a fork and stir gently.

After 4 to 6 hours, serve or store in an airtight container

In a large microwave-safe bowl, whisk the evaporated milk and cornstarch together until well combined. Microwave on high for 1 minute. Remove from the microwave, whisk thoroughly, and then return to the microwave for another minute. Remove, whisk again, and microwave for 30 seconds to 1 minute more, until the mixture is scalding. Carefully remove from the microwave and whisk until most of the steam is gone.

Slowly add the cheese, whisking or blending with an immersion blender, until all the cheese is melted and smooth. Add salt, garlic powder, turmeric, paprika, and yellow mustard. Serve immediately or store in an airtight container and refrigerate. The sauce can be reheated gently in the microwave 30 seconds at a time.

To assemble the nachos: On a large plate make a base layer of corn chips and cover generously with nacho cheese. Add about ½ cup of chili beans or more as desired and sprinkle with onion and jalapenos. Drizzle with a little more nacho cheese.

TIP: Steer clear of pre-shredded cheeses. They're full of anticaking agents that prevent the cheese from blending well.

RORY: *"Since when does the trucker crowd off Highway 84 come through Stars Hollow?"*

DEAN: *"Since we installed an Icee machine."*

APPLE & CHERRY
Turnovers

Some of the best desserts come from the freezer, and apple and cherry turnovers are no exception. This homemade version might not have that same hint of back-of-the-freezer taste to it, but they're fresh and warm out of the oven, and you can always freeze the extras if that's your thing. Do we want the apple turnovers or the cherry? Yes.

YIELD: 12 turnovers

FOR THE APPLE FILLING
2 crisp apples, peeled, cored, and diced
2 tablespoons lemon juice
¼ cup brown sugar, packed
½ teaspoon cinnamon
¼ teaspoon salt
2 tablespoons unsalted butter

FOR THE CHERRY FILLING
½ tablespoon xanthan gum
½ cup sugar
2 cups frozen cherries
2 tablespoons lemon juice

FOR THE TURNOVERS
One 2-sheet package frozen puff pastry
1 egg whisked with 1 tablespoon water, for egg wash
Additional granulated sugar, for topping

To make the apple filling, in a medium-sized bowl, stir together the chopped apples, lemon juice, brown sugar, cinnamon, and salt. Set aside.

In a large skillet over medium-high heat, melt the butter until just beginning to foam and add the apple mixture. Bring the mixture to a boil, reduce to a simmer, and cook until apples are tender and syrup coats the back of a spoon, about 10 minutes.

Remove from heat and allow to cool completely. Note: The filling can be made a day ahead and refrigerated in an airtight container.

To make the cherry filling, mix the xanthan gum with the sugar. In a medium saucepan over medium heat, combine the cherries, sugar mixture, and lemon juice.

Bring mixture to a boil, smashing cherries until mixture is thickened and coats the back of a spoon, around 10 minutes. Remove from heat.

Allow to cool completely. Note: Filling can be made a day ahead and refrigerated in an airtight container.

To make the turnovers, allow both fillings to cool completely while defrosting puff pastry according to package directions.

To assemble, roll out each sheet of pastry to approximately 10-by-15 inches. Cut the pastry sheets into 5-by-5-inch squares to make a total of six squares, keeping each one as even as possible.

Allow the pastry to chill at least 15 minutes before finishing assembly.

In the center of each square, place approximately ¼ cup of apple or cherry filling. Use a pastry brush to brush egg wash on two sides of the square and fold the other side over, creating a triangle. Crimp closed with a fork.

Preheat the oven to 425°F. Chill turnovers for 20 minutes and then bake for 15 to 20 minutes or freeze on a cookie sheet and transfer to an airtight container.

Frozen turnovers can be baked at 425°F for 15 to 20 minutes.

HOMEMADE
Toaster Pastries

All Lorelai has ever wanted is some freedom and independence from her parents, and she has used many things, including her breakfast, as an act of rebellion against them. When Lorelai breaks up with Luke, she has an existential crisis and questions whether she actually loves toaster pastries, one of her main breakfast staples, or if she loves that her parents hate that she loves toaster pastries. Why not both? You can almost taste the freedom in these strawberry-jam filled breakfast treats.

YIELD: About 6 toaster pastries

FOR THE FILLING
Approximately ⅓ cup strawberry jam

FOR THE TART
2 cups all-purpose flour, plus more as needed

1 tablespoon wheat flour

1½ sticks cold unsalted butter, diced

2 tablespoons light brown sugar

1 teaspoon kosher salt

3 tablespoons sour cream, divided, plus more as needed

2 tablespoons shortening

½ teaspoon vanilla extract

1 large egg, beaten with about a tablespoon of water, for the egg wash

FOR THE ICING
2 tablespoons milk

¼ teaspoon vanilla extract

¾ cup to 1 cup powdered sugar, sifted

To make the tart, add the all-purpose flour, wheat flour, butter, brown sugar, and salt to the bowl of a food processor. Pulse until thoroughly combined and the texture is mealy. Add 2 tablespoons of sour cream and pulse a few times. Add 1 more tablespoon of sour cream, the shortening, and vanilla. Pulse until the dough combines and begins to form into a ball. The texture should be smooth, not dry or sticky. The dough should hold its shape when pressed between your fingers. If the dough feels dry, add a tablespoon or two of sour cream.

Form the dough into a disk and refrigerate for 30 minutes.

Remove the dough from the refrigerator. On a lightly floured work surface, roll the dough out to about ⅛ inch thick. Using a cookie cutter or a knife, cut out 3-by-4½-inch rectangles. Gather the scraps and reroll as needed.

On half of the rectangles, spread about 1 tablespoon of jam, leaving the edges exposed. Using a pastry brush, brush egg wash along each edge and top with a second rectangle. Use a fork to crimp the edges together and "dock" the top.

Preheat oven to 375°F. Arrange the tarts on the prepared sheet tray and refrigerate until the dough is firm, 15 to 20 minutes.

To make the icing, in a medium bowl, whisk together the milk, vanilla, and powdered sugar to create a thick white glue-like icing. Stir to combine. Add in more powdered sugar or milk as needed to create the appropriate texture.

Bake the tarts until light golden brown and cooked throughout, 30 to 40 minutes. Let cool so they are warm, but not hot, about 10 minutes. Spoon 1 teaspoon of icing onto the top of each tart. Spread the icing as it begins drip, keeping it on the pastry. Immediately sprinkle with the sanding sugar, if desired, while the tarts are still warm. Serve warm or room temperature. Store in an airtight container. Tarts can be reheated in the oven, if not iced, at 350°F for 5 to 7 minutes.

BEST WAYS TO

Order Takeout, Reheat Takeout, or —— (If You're into Cooking) Bake Frozen Things ——

Ordering takeout can be an art form, as Lorelai helps Rory and the dorm discover at Yale. Make sure that you have a good selection of menus at the ready. The balance comes from a combination of speed of delivery, cuteness of the delivery person, and last and almost least important . . . food quality. Always make sure to order at least twice as much food as the people present can eat. First, you never know when an unexpected guest will show up wanting egg rolls or spicy shrimp, and second of all, a Gilmore plans ahead.

Tomorrow has arrived, and you are blessed with the bounty of last night's takeout! Leftovers were made to be eaten cold, but if you insist on reheating, here are some tips:

- Dishes, like chow mein, cashew chicken, or soy pudding will benefit from proper microwave reheating. Place the food on a microwave-safe plate, or in a bowl, cover with a damp paper towel, and microwave for 1 minute. Carefully remove from the microwave, stir, check the temperature, re-cover, and microwave for 1 minute more or as necessary.

Items like pizza and egg rolls never fare well in the microwave, so if you must reheat, use your oven. Heat the oven to 375°F with a cookie sheet inside of it. (Note: Refer to the user manual for instructions on how to turn the oven on, or just fiddle with all the knobs and buttons until it feels hot.) When the oven is heated, place the leftovers on the cookie sheet and bake for 5 to 7 minutes or until the desired effect. Crispy? Melty? Gooey?

And cooking delicious frozen foods doesn't have to be a chore if you follow these easy tips:

- First read your package directions to find out important information like oven temperature and how long you're going to suffer hunger until your food is done. If it's going to take more than 30 minutes, you may want to order some takeout (see above) to hold you over until it's done cooking.

- Next preheat your oven. Food should not go in before the oven has been checked for random household items, spare purses, or other non-food related things. If the food you're cooking should turn out crispy, such as French fries, tater tots, or pizza, let the cookie sheets preheat with the oven. Foods like a casserole, turnover, or frozen lasagna should not go in the oven until it has reached the prescribed temperature.

LORELAI: *"Well I'm a leftover girl. I'll just have the burgers tonight and the Chinese food during the week."*

LUKE: *"Then you should've just ordered the Chinese fresh tomorrow instead of tonight."*

LORELAI: *"I don't like fresh Chinese food. I like stale Chinese food!"*

CHAPTER Five

Beyond Stars Hallow

Most of us would never leave Stars Hollow if we didn't have to, but Lorelai and Rory do venture out into the world sometimes—mainly because, well, Emily says they have to. Friday Night Dinners offer an entirely different kind of culinary education than Lorelai and Rory are used to. Did you know that there's more to making a strudel than pulling it out of the freezer and sticking it in the toaster? Did you even know Richard Gilmore can pull off a pasta dish?

Food is an important part of Rory's evolutionary journey into a Yale woman as well. Yale Rory goes on Spring Break. Yale-dropout Rory plans DAR events and wears tweed and serves salmon puffs and, oh, my gosh, she's turning into a mini Emily. Back-to-Yale-again Rory likes tapas. That's huge growth from the girl who used to live off donuts and Red Vines.

FRIDAY NIGHT DINNER

With Emily & Richard

Friday Night Dinners are the backbone of the Gilmore Girls' story. Dinners at the Gilmore mansion have been the setting for some nice, warm family moments—and for big blowouts, crushing revelations, betrayal, resentment, revenge, and a whole lot of repressed tears. But, hey, at least the food is good. Or, it would be, if the maid (whatever her name is) prepared it right.

POT ROAST, POTATOES, & ROLLS

Even with the greatest chefs and most exotic foods at her behest, Rory's dinner of choice is a pot roast with potatoes and rolls. When Emily invites her over for a meal of all her favorite things, Rory is a little suspicious, and rightfully so (it's Emily Gilmore, after all). The dinner is actually an intervention. The Gilmores invited Reverend Boatwright over to give Rory a talk about giving her greatest gift—her virtue—to the right person because she can only give it away once. Sorry Boatwright, that boat has sailed. Oh, well, at least Rory got to enjoy this juicy roast and buttery rolls.

EVERYTHING PARKER HOUSE ROLLS

YIELD: 24 rolls

1½ cups whole milk

½ cup unsalted butter, cut into 8 pieces, plus 2 tablespoons butter, melted

4½ teaspoons active dry yeast

4 cups all-purpose flour

3 tablespoons granulated sugar

1 tablespoon kosher salt

Vegetable oil, for greasing

In a small saucepan over medium heat, combine the milk and butter. Warm until the butter has melted, about 7 minutes. Remove from the heat and let cool until the mixture registers 105° to 115°F on an instant-read thermometer. Add the yeast and stir until dissolved. Let stand for 10 minutes.

In the bowl of a stand mixer fitted with the dough hook, combine the flour, sugar, and kosher salt and beat on low speed until combined, about 30 seconds. Add the milk mixture and continue to beat on low speed until the dough forms a ball, about 1 minute. Increase the speed to medium-low and knead until the dough is smooth and elastic, 4 to 5 minutes. Remove the dough from the mixer bowl, oil the inside of the bowl, and return the dough to the bowl. Cover the bowl tightly with plastic wrap and let the dough rise in a warm place until doubled in size, about 1 hour. Divide the dough in half.

Continues on page 132

Continued from page 131

Grease a 9-by-13-inch baking pan. On a lightly floured work surface, roll each piece of dough into a log 12 inches long. Using a pastry scraper, divide each log into 12 equal pieces. Using the cupped palm of your hand, roll and shape each piece into a taut ball.

Arrange the dough balls in the prepared baking pan, making 4 rows of 6 balls each. Cover the pan tightly with plastic wrap and let the balls rise in a warm place for 30 minutes.

Preheat the oven to 375°F.

Remove the plastic wrap from the pan. Brush the tops of the rolls with the melted butter. Bake until the rolls are golden and an instant-read thermometer inserted into the center of a roll registers 190°F, 18 to 20 minutes.

Invert the rolls onto a wire rack, remove the pan, then turn the rolls right side up onto another rack. Let the rolls cool slightly before serving.

"Oh, yes. You know, Rory, being a young lady comes with many gifts. Your virtue, for example, is a gift, a precious gift. Possibly the most precious gift you possess."

REV. BOATWRIGHT

CLASSIC POT ROAST

YIELD: 6 to 8 servings

5 tablespoons all-purpose flour, divided

Salt and ground pepper

1 beef chuck roast, 3 to 4 pounds

2 tablespoons unsalted butter

2 tablespoons canola oil

4 carrots, 2 finely chopped and 2 cut into 1-inch pieces

1 yellow onion, chopped

1 celery stalk, chopped

3 cups beef stock

3 Yukon Gold potatoes (about 1 pound total weight), peeled and quartered

1 cup frozen pearl onions

½ cup frozen peas

Preheat the oven to 325°F.

In a large bowl, stir together 3 tablespoons of the flour, 1 teaspoon salt, and ½ teaspoon pepper. Turn the roast in the seasoned flour, shaking off any excess.

In a large Dutch oven or oven-safe pan over medium-high heat, melt the butter with the oil. Add the roast and cook, turning occasionally, until browned on all sides, about 10 minutes. Transfer the roast to a plate.

Pour off all but 2 tablespoons of the fat in the pot. Add the chopped carrots, onion, and celery and sauté over medium-high heat until softened, about 5 minutes. Stir in the remaining 2 tablespoons flour and cook for about 1 minute. Pour in the stock, bring to a boil, and deglaze the pan, stirring to dislodge any browned bits on the pan bottom.

Add the roast back to the Dutch oven, cover, and bake, turning the roast occasionally, until the meat is very tender, about 3 hours. Remove the pot from the oven and transfer the roast to a platter.

Strain the cooking liquid through a fine-mesh sieve into a heatproof bowl; discard the solids. Skim any fat from the surface of the cooking liquid. Return the roast and liquid to the pot and stir in the potatoes, carrot pieces, and pearl onions. Cover and bake for 30 minutes. Uncover and stir in the peas. Re-cover and bake until all the vegetables are tender, about 15 minutes longer.

Transfer the roast to a cutting board, tent with aluminum foil, and let rest for about 10 minutes. To serve, cut the roast against the grain into slices and divide among warmed individual shallow bowls. Using a large spoon, divide the vegetables and cooking liquid among the plates. Season the vegetables with salt and pepper and serve right away.

Slow-cooker method: Place the browned roast and broth mixture in the slow cooker, cover, and cook for 8 hours on low. Strain and skim the liquids; cook for 1 hour longer with the vegetables, adding the peas during the last 15 minutes of cooking.

The best pot roast: Many believe that chuck roast, a muscular shoulder section of the steer, makes the best pot roast. Not actually roasted at all but braised in a savory cooking liquid, the beef becomes meltingly tender and juicy after long, slow cooking in a covered pot.

CHOCOLATE CAKE
& Coffee

If you can make it to the end of a Friday Night Dinner, you deserve an award, and this dessert will make the whole night worth it. The rich, fudgy chocolate cake is frosted with a buttercream frosting and filled with a raspberry Bavarian cream. Enjoy with your favorite strong coffee because you need to stay alert. You haven't beaten the game yet—there's always time for a Gilmore to throw a last-minute verbal sucker punch.

YIELD: 8 to 10 servings

FOR THE CAKE:

3 cups all-purpose flour

1½ cups unsweetened cocoa powder

3 cups sugar

2 teaspoon baking powder

2 teaspoon baking soda

1½ cup milk

½ cup vegetable oil

4 eggs

1 tablespoon vanilla extract

2 cups very hot water

FOR THE RASPBERRY BAVARIAN CREAM:

1 cup raspberries, plus extra for garnish

2 tablespoons lemon juice

½ cup sugar

1 envelope (2¼ teaspoons) unflavored gelatin

2 cups heavy whipping cream

FOR THE BUTTERCREAM FROSTING

10 ounces bittersweet chocolate

5 tablespoons heavy whipping cream

6 egg whites

1¼ cups granulated sugar

½ teaspoon cream of tartar

2 cups (4 sticks) unsalted butter, softened

Candy thermometer

To make the cake, prepare two 9-inch cake pans by lining the bottom with parchment paper cut to fit. Preheat the oven to 350°F.

Sift the flour, cocoa powder, sugar, baking powder, and baking soda together into the bowl of a stand mixer.

Whisk the milk, oil, eggs, and vanilla together in a small bowl or measuring cup.

On medium-high, mix the wet ingredients into the dry ingredients until well combined, 3 to 5 minutes. Make sure to periodically stop the mixer and scrape up from the bottom and down the sides.

Add the hot water in a slow steady stream, mixing on low until well combined. The batter will be very runny. Make sure to periodically stop the mixer and scrape up from the bottom and down the sides.

Split batter between the two prepared cake pans. Bake for 25 to 30 minutes or until a cake tester comes out mostly clean. A few fudgy crumbs are okay.

Allow to cool in the pan for 15 minutes and then gently release the edges with an offset spatula. Allow to cool completely on a wire rack.

RORY: *"Okay, our house is burning down, and you can save the cake or me. What do you choose?"*

LORELAI: *"Well that's not fair. The cake doesn't have legs."*

Trim each cake level if necessary and cut into even layers, creating 4 layers about 1 inch thick.

To make the raspberry Bavarian cream, in a small saucepan, combine the raspberries, lemon juice, and sugar. Bring to a boil over medium-high heat, stirring frequently for 2 or 3 minutes to break down raspberries.

Strain raspberries through a fine sieve discarding seeds and pulp, and return to the saucepan. Sprinkle gelatin over the top and allow it to bloom for 2 to 3 minutes. Return saucepan to medium-high heat and bring to a boil, whisking continuously until gelatin is completely dissolved. Decant to a heatproof bowl and chill in the refrigerator.

In the bowl of the stand mixer, whip the heavy cream until stiff peaks form. Fold the cooled raspberry mixture into whipping cream. Refrigerate until ready to assemble the cake.

To make the buttercream frosting, in a microwave-safe bowl, combine the chocolate and heavy whipping cream. Microwave for 1 minute. Leave undisturbed for 5 minutes then stir until smooth. Set aside.

Place a pot or pan of water on the stove, large enough to fit the bowl of your stand mixer. Fill partially with water and bring to a boil.

Place the egg whites, sugar, and cream of tartar into the bowl of the stand mixer and whisk together. Place the bowl into the boiling water, whisk constantly to dissolve the sugar, and bring to 160°F.

Remove the bowl from the stove and use the whisk attachment to whip the egg white mixture on high until stiff peaks form and the bowl is cool to the touch.

Reduce mixer speed to medium-low and add the butter 1 to 2 tablespoons at a time until all the butter is incorporated.

Add the chocolate mixture and whisk on low until thoroughly combined.

Use immediately or refrigerate in an airtight container. Note: Buttercream must be brought to room temperature before stirring and using.

To assemble the cake, fill a piping bag with chocolate buttercream and snip about ½ inch from the end. Pipe a wall along the outer edge of the bottom cake layer and fill the center with about 1 cup of the Bavarian cream. Spread into an even layer. Top with an additional cake layer and repeat until all four layers are stacked. Leave the top free of filling.

Working with a large offset spatula and the rest of the buttercream, pile frosting on the top and work it down the sides. Create a swirled texture with the back of a spoon. Garnish with fresh raspberries.

DARK CHOCOLATE
Pudding

Lorelai loves pudding. She *worships* pudding. She has a bowl of it up on the mantel at home with the Virgin Mary, a glass of wine, and a dollar bill next to it. Needless to say, she was thrown off when Emily served it for dessert. What, was she trying to be nice or something? Very suspicious behavior from Emily Gilmore. You'll worship this pudding too, especially if you top it with a dollop of fresh whipped cream.

YIELD: 2 servings

FOR THE PUDDING
¾ cup granulated sugar
1/3 cup cornstarch
¼ teaspoon salt
4 cups milk
3 ounces unsweetened chocolate, chopped
1 teaspoon pure vanilla extract
Whipped cream for serving
Shaved chocolate for garnish

FOR THE WHIPPED CREAM
1 cup cold heavy cream
4 teaspoons sugar
1 teaspoon pure vanilla extract

To make the pudding, in a heatproof bowl, whisk together the sugar, cornstarch, and salt. Set aside.

In a saucepan over medium heat, warm the milk until small bubbles appear around the edge of the pan. Add the chocolate and stir until melted, about 1 minute. Remove from the heat and stir in the vanilla.

Carefully ladle about one-quarter of the chocolate mixture into the sugar mixture and whisk until smooth. Add the remaining chocolate mixture and again whisk until smooth. Pour the combined mixtures back into the saucepan and place over medium heat. Cook, stirring constantly, until the pudding begins to thicken, scraping the pan well with a heat-resistant spatula to make sure it doesn't burn. Continue to cook, stirring constantly, until very thick, about 2 minutes.

Ladle the pudding into bowls, place a piece of plastic wrap directly on top, and let cool for at least 30 minutes. Serve right away or cover and refrigerate for up to 4 hours. Top each serving with whipped cream and chocolate shavings.

To make the whipped cream, in a chilled bowl, combine the heavy cream, sugar, and vanilla. Using a whisk, beat until soft peaks form. Alternatively, using an electric mixer, beat on medium-high speed until soft peaks form.

If you want to use a pastry (piping) bag to pipe the cream, beat until stiff peaks form.

Use the whipped cream right away or cover and refrigerate until serving time. Whip slightly, if needed, before using.

GIN MARTINI
No Onion

When Emily gets mad at Lorelai for cherry-picking which Friday Night Dinners she attends, she makes her feelings clear by boxing Lorelai out of the dinner with Logan and Rory and making her feel unwanted. Emily brings on some of her best psychological warfare in forgetting that Lorelai's preferred drink is not a sidecar, not a vodka martini with a twist, but a gin martini with an olive (hold the passive-aggressive onion).

YIELD: 1 martini

3 ounces gin
½ ounce dry vermouth
1 martini olive

In a cocktail shaker filled with ice, combine the gin and vermouth. Cover, shake vigorously, and strain into a chilled martini glass. Garnish with the olive (not an onion!).

*"Pretty much every one of the other 8,000 times
I've had a drink here, it's been a martini."*

LORELAI

THE RORY

Drink

Every privileged twenty-one-year-old needs three things: birthday party invitations adorned with pearls, individual chocolate boxes for every party guest, and their own signature cocktail. Introducing: The Rory!

Emily's chef concocted a drink that was sweet, pink, served in a martini glass even though it's not a martini, and really, *really* pink. Since the guest reviews of that drink were less than favorable, we revamped The Rory and created a lovely raspberry-rose mocktail that you can also turn into a cocktail by adding 2 ounces of gin to the shaker. It's every bit as festive—and every bit as pink.

YIELD: 1 drink

FOR THE RASPBERRY-ROSE SYRUP
1 cup water
1 cup granulated sugar
1½ cups raspberries
4 drops rose water

FOR THE COCKTAIL
2 teaspoons meringue powder
2 tablespoons of water
¾ ounce fresh lemon juice
¾ ounce raspberry-rose syrup
2 ounces of ginger ale
Rose petals, for garnish
Pink sanding sugar for rim, optional

To make the raspberry-rose syrup, in a small saucepan, heat the water and sugar over medium heat until the sugar dissolves. Remove from the heat, add the raspberries, and mash them. Add the rose water and let steep for 2 hours or overnight. Strain through a fine-mesh strainer, pressing the raspberry solids to extract all the juices. Store the syrup in a sealed jar in the refrigerator for up to 2 weeks.

If rimming the glass, fill a shallow plate with sanding sugar, use a lemon wedge to moisten the edge of each glass, and then dip the edges in the sugar to coat. Let stand while making cocktail.

To make the cocktail, combine the meringue powder and water in a cocktail shaker and stir to combine. Add lemon juice and raspberry-rose syrup, shake vigorously with ice, and strain into a martini or coupe glass. Top with ginger ale and garnish with rose petals.

"Oh, it tasted pink ... I mean, like, really tasted really pink. Like pink-pink. Yuck!"

LUKE

EMILY'S TAILGATE
Bloody Marys

Emily Gilmore has a reputation for being, say, a little rigid, but once a year she lets her hair down for the big Harvard Yale football game. She drinks from a flask, wears dirty buttons, and mixes an incredibly strong Bloody Mary. Like really strong, like don't-stand-within-six-feet-of-this-drink-and-drive strong. Our recipe starts as a virgin Bloody Mary, but you can add the vodka as sparingly (or not) as you'd like. For the cocktail version, stir in 2 cups of vodka to combine with the other ingredients before decanting into glasses or tumblers. Oh, and one last thing: go to hell, Harvard! You too, Pennilyn Lott!

YIELD: 6 servings

1 lemon, halved

4 cups tomato juice

2 teaspoons freshly grated horseradish

2 teaspoons A1 Steak Sauce or Worcestershire sauce

2 teaspoons celery salt

1 teaspoon cayenne pepper

½ teaspoon paprika

Freshly ground black pepper

Ice cubes

6 celery ribs with leaves

6 long, thin radish slices

Squeeze the juice from the lemon halves into a large pitcher. Add the tomato juice, horseradish, A1 sauce, celery salt, cayenne, paprika, and a few grinds of black pepper and stir until thoroughly combined.

Fill six rocks glasses or tumblers with ice and pour the mixture over the ice, dividing it evenly. Garnish with the celery ribs and radish slices and serve.

RICHARD: *"You have been working on your Bloody Marys for an hour now."*

EMILY: *"Rome wasn't built in a day. Taste that, Lorelai."*

LORELAI: *"Ugh! Hooyah!"*

MASHED BANANAS
On Toast

Nobody ever accused Emily Gilmore of being too maternal. Her approach to motherhood has always been cold, but when Lorelai hurts her back and needs some TLC, Emily shows love the best way she knows how: the mashed bananas spread over toast that she used to make whenever little Lorelai was sick. This snack is warm enough to melt Emily's icy exterior, at least for one night. And, sure, maybe it was disgusting, and maybe Lorelai and Emily both spit it out, but we tweaked the recipe with some vanilla and cinnamon and turned it into a delicious and simple snack.

Yield: 2 servings

1 ripe banana
Juice of ½ lime
1 teaspoon vanilla paste
¼ teaspoon cinnamon
2 pieces of whole wheat bread, toasted

In a small bowl, combine the banana and lime juice. Smash with a fork until the banana is broken up. Add vanilla paste and cinnamon and stir to combine thoroughly.

Spread on toast and serve.

"Mom, I think somebody already ate that."

LORELAI

LOGAN'S
Surprise Gazpacho

Rory was thrilled when Logan surprised her with a romantic evening during his impromptu visit from London: a fake meteor shower on the rooftop, twinkling fairy lights, an oaky red wine. The tapas, flan, and gazpacho were just the icing on the cake. This gazpacho recipe has a garden-fresh flavor that tastes like it's straight out of Ibiza (the restaurant, not the island).

YIELD: 8 to 10 servings

2½ pounds fresh ripe plum tomatoes, seeded and roughly chopped

1 English cucumber (about ½ pound), peeled, seeded, and chopped into 1-to-2-inch chunks, plus more for garnish

1 small or ½ a large red bell pepper, seeded and cored with membranes removed, chopped into 1-to-2-inch chunks, plus more for garnish

3 to 4 cloves garlic, peeled

4 tablespoons red wine vinegar

6 slices good quality white bread, crust removed, divided

1 cup unseasoned tomato juice or puree

¼ cup good quality olive oil, plus 2 tablespoons for croutons

1 teaspoon kosher salt

1 tablespoon butter

Place the tomato, cucumber, and pepper in a medium bowl.

Chop the garlic in the blender. Add the tomato, pepper, and cucumber in batches with two tablespoons of vinegar at a time. Puree thoroughly between each addition.

Soak 2 slices bread in the tomato juice and then add to the blender and puree again. Add the salt and puree to combine.

With the blender on low, drizzle in the olive oil until it is all incorporated. Turn the blender back to high for 30 seconds to a minute to puree until smooth.

Chill in an airtight container at least 4 hours or overnight.

To make the croutons, cut the remaining 4 pieces of bread into cubes. In a large sauté pan, heat the remaining 2 tablespoons olive oil and the butter. When the butter has foamed, add the bread cubes. Stir frequently to prevent burning and cook until well toasted, 3 to 5 minutes. Let cool and store in an airtight container until serving.

To serve the gazpacho, slice swizzle sticks of cucumber and red bell pepper. Pour gazpacho into short cafe glasses, top with a few croutons, and garnish with cucumber and pepper. Serve with small spoons.

LOGAN: *"Doesn't take much to make you happy, does it?"*

RORY: *"Not when you're on the same continent!"*

LOBSTER
Pot Pie

Did you know you can't thermidor a chicken, but you can pot pie a lobster? Emily was less than impressed with Lorelai's presentation during her tasting with Independence Catering, but Sookie's Lobster Pot Pie won her over. How could it not? This Lobster Pot Pie has a flaky golden crust and bubbles over with a piping hot creamy lobster filling.

YIELD: 6 servings

3 ears corn

1 tablespoon olive oil

2 tablespoons butter, plus more for greasing

1 cup chopped celery, preferably heart with leaves

1 cup frozen pearl onions

½ cup white wine

1 sprig fresh dill

2 raw lobster tails and reserved tail meat from Lobster Bisque (page 57), or 4 raw lobster tails

2½ cups vegetable broth, divided

2 tablespoons all-purpose flour

3 to 4 small yellow potatoes, quartered

1 cup frozen peas

2 sheets of puff pastry defrosted but chilling in the refrigerator.

Egg wash

SPECIAL TOOLS

Six 8-ounce ramekins

Lobster cookie cutter and egg wash (see page 166 for instructions on making an egg wash

Preheat oven to 400°F.

Coat each ear of corn in the olive oil and roast for 15 to 17 minutes or until tender and starting to brown. Allow to cool and then cut the corn from the cob and set aside.

Melt the butter in a large sauté pan with a tight-fitting lid. Sauté the celery and onions until starting to brown, 3 to 4 minutes.

Add the wine and sprig of dill to the pan and cook for 2 to 3 minutes, deglazing the pan as you go.

Place the raw lobster tails in the pan with ½ cup of the broth, cover, and steam for 5 to 7 minutes or until shells are bright red and flesh is opaque white.

Remove the lobster tails and sprig of dill from the pan and set aside. Whisk in the flour.

Add the remaining broth and potatoes to the sauté pan. Simmer for 7 to 10 minutes or until the potatoes are just tender.

Remove from the heat and stir in the peas and corn kernels. Set aside.

Using kitchen shears or a sharp knife cut down the top of the lobster tail and remove the meat. Cut into bite-sized pieces and stir into the filling mixture.

Butter the ramekins and split the filling mixture between the ramekins, making sure everyone has some lobster.

Remove the puff pastry from the refrigerator and use the cookie cutter to cut two lobsters for each top. Place the pastry lobsters across the top of the ramekin facing opposite each other and "gripping" the sides of the ramekin. Brush with egg wash and bake for 15 to 20 minutes or until puff pastry is golden brown.

Let cool for 5 minutes and then serve.

"Hey, can you thermidor other foods? You know, fish thermidor. Spam thermidor, enchiladas thermidor?"

LORELAI

TRIX'S
Spiced Nuts

When Richard's mother, the original Lorelai, comes to visit, Emily gets a taste of what it's like to have an Emily of her own, but even Trix loved these mixed nuts. They're nutty, salty, spicy, and umami-y all at once. If you have company, make sure to serve them with a plate and napkins to avoid the wrath of any hypercritical dinner guests.

YIELD: 2 cups, 6 to 8 servings

1 cup raw almonds
½ cup raw cashews
½ cup raw pistachios
2 tablespoons tamari
2 tablespoons pure maple syrup
2 tablespoons sesame seeds
¼ teaspoon cayenne pepper
½ teaspoon flaky sea salt

Preheat the oven to 350°F. Line a baking sheet with parchment paper or a silicone baking mat.

Spread the almonds, cashews, and pistachios in a single layer on the prepared baking sheet and toast for 5 minutes.

Meanwhile, in a large bowl, whisk together the tamari, maple syrup, sesame seeds, and cayenne.

Remove the nuts from the oven, add to the bowl with the tamari mixture, and toss to coat evenly. Spread the nuts in a single layer on the baking sheet and sprinkle with the sea salt. Bake until the nuts are lightly browned and smell toasty, about 12 minutes. Transfer the parchment paper to a wire rack and let the nuts cool for 10 minutes. Using a spatula, transfer the nuts to a bowl, breaking apart any clumps.

Store in an airtight container at room temperature for up to 3 days.

"So Lorelai, since I've seen you last, you've grown up, gotten pregnant out of wedlock, raised a child, and still haven't bothered to get married. Have I left anything out?"

TRIX

JOHNNY MACHETTE'S
Pasta Casserole

Even a kept man like Richard Gilmore likes to commandeer the kitchen sometimes. This colorful creamy casserole is from an old secret family recipe. Young Dickie's grandmother would make it for him when he came home crying after losing a cricket tournament. Like all the best comfort foods, Richard recommends Johnny Machette's Pasta Casserole be served in a heap.

YIELD: 6 to 8 servings

1 pound bowtie pasta

2 tablespoons vegetable oil, divided

1 zucchini squash, sliced and cut into half moons

2 small yellow gooseneck squashes, sliced and cut into half moons

1 small onion, diced

1 red bell pepper, diced

1 teaspoon of salt

Fresh ground pepper to taste

1 cup milk

11 ounces condensed mushroom soup

½ teaspoon smoked paprika

10 ounces water-packed tuna, drained, and broken up

1 sleeve saltine crackers (about 5 ounces) crushed to a course crumb

3 tablespoons butter, melted, plus more to butter the dish

Preheat the oven to 350°F.

Butter a 9-by-13-inch casserole dish. In a large pot with salted water, cook the pasta according to the package directions.

While the pasta is cooking, in a large sauté pan over medium-high heat, add 1½ teaspoon of the oil. Working in batches, cook the squash in single layers until brown on both sides, about 3 to 5 minutes. Add a bit more oil with each batch of squash. When each batch is done, transfer to the casserole dish. Repeat until all the squash is cooked.

In the pan, add the remaining oil, onion, pepper, and salt. Sauté until the onion is translucent and the pepper has softened, 5 to 7 minutes. Transfer to the casserole dish.

In a medium saucepan over medium heat, add the milk, condensed soup, paprika, and black pepper. Stir until well combined and thickened slightly.

When the pasta is ready, drain and return to the pot. Pour the soup mixture over the pasta and stir to combine.

Add the tuna and all the vegetables to the pasta and stir to combine. Add back into the casserole dish.

In a medium bowl, combine the cracker crumbs with the melted butter and stir until the crackers are coated in the butter.

Top the casserole with the cracker mixture and bake for 20 to 25 minutes until bubbly and golden brown on top. Serve immediately.

"My gran used to make this for me whenever I was feeling a little sad. You know, if my cricket team lost or a girl I fancied turned up her nose at me."

RICHARD

SALMON
Puffs

If there's one thing Emily Gilmore likes, it's being in control. So, when Rory takes the reins of the DAR's USO charity event and goes rogue with the menu, Emily begins to unravel. And who can blame her? Rory isn't serving salmon puffs. They've *never* not served salmon puffs! They're the perfect canape: sweet, smokey, sophisticated, and expensive.

YIELD: About 24 puffs

FOR THE PASTRY PUFFS
½ recipe of choux paste (Pâte à Choux, page 116) with the sugar omitted

FOR THE FILLING
4 ounces cream cheese, softened

¼ cup creme fraiche

1 teaspoon fresh squeezed lemon juice

1 tablespoon capers, roughly chopped

1½ ounces smoked salmon, finely chopped

2 teaspoon fresh snipped chives, plus more for garnish

Fresh ground pepper to taste

To make the pastry puffs, preheat the oven to 400°F.

Line two cookie sheets with parchment. Tip: Using a bit of choux paste to stick down the corners of the parchment paper will help keep it in place while piping.

Fill a large pastry bag fitted with a plain ½-inch tip with the choux paste. Pipe about 1-inch balls spaced 2 inches apart onto the cookie sheets. Dip your finger in water and gently smooth out the tip left when you lift the bag.

Bake for 10 minutes and then reduce the oven temperature to 350°F. Bake for another 20 to 25 minutes or until golden brown and firm to the touch.

With a sharp skewer or the tip of a paring knife, poke a small hole into the bottom of each puff and place back on the cookie sheet upside down (or on their side) to allow the steam to escape while cooling. Store in an airtight container until filling.

To make the filling, with a hand mixer on medium, blend the cream cheese, creme fraiche, and lemon juice together until well combined and fluffy. Fold in the capers, smoked salmon, and chives. Add fresh ground pepper to taste.

Load the filling into a pastry bag with a ¼-inch tip and fill puffs from the bottom. Do not overfill.

Place a tiny dot or swipe of filling cream on the top of each puff and sprinkle with more snipped chives. Serve immediately or refrigerate in an airtight container for up to 4 hours.

"We've never not served salmon puffs. Not in 25 years have we staged an event without salmon puffs."

EMILY

ROSA'S
Lamb Sandwich

When Rory sought refuge at her grandparents' house after fighting with Lorelai, she got a taste of what life on the other side looks like, and brown bag school lunches look a little different when they're done Richard and Emily style. Leftovers from a fabulous leg of herb and mustard crusted lamb can be thrown together, nay orchestrated, into a delicious cold sandwich. Don't forget to DEMAND a slice of strudel on the side!

YIELD: 6 to 8 servings

FOR THE LAMB
2 racks of lamb, about 1½ pounds and 8 chops each, trimmed of all but a thin layer of fat
Kosher salt and freshly ground pepper
1 tablespoon olive oil
¾ cup fine fresh breadcrumbs
1 clove garlic, minced
1 teaspoon chopped fresh thyme
½ teaspoon chopped fresh rosemary
2 tablespoons butter, melted
3 tablespoons Dijon mustard

FOR THE SANDWICH
1 sourdough or ciabatta roll
1 tablespoon whole grain mustard
Drizzle of olive oil
½ cup baby arugula leaves
¼ crumbled feta cheese

Preheat the oven to 400°F. Season the lamb racks with salt and pepper. Heat the olive oil in a large sauté pan over medium-high heat. Sear the lamb, one rack at a time, browning on each side (about 2½ minutes per side). Using a pair of tongs, hold each rack upright and sear the ends, about 20 seconds each. The racks should look golden. Transfer the racks to a 13-by-9-inch baking dish.

Stir together the breadcrumbs, garlic, thyme, rosemary, and melted butter in a bowl. Season with a pinch of salt and mix well. Brush or smear the seared lamb thoroughly with a thin layer of mustard. Sprinkle the bread-crumb mixture over the surface of the lamb, gently pressing the mixture onto the lamb so that it adheres.

Roast the lamb until an instant-read thermometer inserted into the center of the meat but not touching bone registers 120°F for rare, about 20 minutes, or 130°F for medium-rare, 25 to 30 minutes. (The temperature of the meat will continue to rise outside of the oven.) Transfer the lamb to a cutting board or serving platter. Allow to rest for 10 minutes to allow the juices to redistribute before slicing into chops and serving.

Leftover lamb can be chilled, sliced thin and used in a sandwich. If making a sandwich, thinly slice the lamb chop. Split the roll in half, spread mustard on one side, and drizzle olive oil on the other. Place sliced lamb on the mustard side and scatter the feta chunks over it. Place the arugula on the second roll piece and drizzle with a bit more olive oil. Put the two halves together, press gently, and cut in half on the angle.

EMILY: *"So do you get your lunch at school or do you bring it with you? Because Rosa made a fabulous leg of lamb yesterday. I bet it'd make a wonderful sandwich."*

RICHARD: *"Take her up on that. It is good. And demand a slice of strudel."*

ROSA'S
Strudel

Ahh, strudel. Rory declined the offer to have Rosa whip her up some toaster pastries after her sleepover at Richard and Emily's, but she wasn't about to turn down some of Rosa's strudel in her brown bag lunch. And, anyway, what is a strudel if not a fancy toaster pastry? This dessert has a thin, flaky pastry wrapped around a sweet apple filling, and believe it or not, it's just as good as the frozen pastries Lorelai usually defrosts for breakfast.

YIELD: 10 to 12 servings

FOR THE DOUGH
2 cups all-purpose flour
1 egg
½ stick of butter, melted, divided.
1 teaspoon sugar
Pinch salt
½ cup warm water

FOR THE FILLING
2 pounds apples
2 teaspoon lemon juice
½ cup granulated sugar
1 teaspoon cinnamon
2 teaspoons vanilla paste
¾ breadcrumbs, fresh, coarse, toasted

Line a baking sheet with parchment paper.

To make the dough, in the bowl of a stand mixer fitted with a dough hook, combine together the flour, egg, 2 tablespoons of the melted butter, sugar, salt, and water until a dough is formed. Knead the dough by hand until it is silky, no longer sticky, and springs back when pressed with your finger. Form the dough into a ball, brush very lightly with more of the melted butter, and wrap in plastic wrap. Leave in a warm place to rest for 45 minutes to an hour.

While the dough is resting, prepare the filling ingredients. Peel, core, and thinly slice the apples, and place them in a large bowl, yielding about 8 cups. Toss them with the lemon juice and have standing by. Mix the sugar, cinnamon, and vanilla paste together until well combined, have standing by.

When the dough has rested, with a rolling pin, roll out the dough on a clean, damp dish towel as thin as you can. Remove any watches or jewelry. Gently stretch and pull the dough small sections at a time until it is as thin possible. You should be able to see the pattern of the fabric through the dough.

Preheat the oven to 400°F.

Cover a rimmed baking sheet with a silicone baking mat or parchment paper. If necessary, re-melt the butter. Brush the entire surface of the dough with a thin layer of butter. Leaving a 3-inch border at the bottom and around the sides of the dough, sprinkle the breadcrumbs evenly over the bottom third of the dough. Mix the apples with the sugar mixture and scatter them in an even layer over the breadcrumbs.

Use the cloth to roll the strudel over and over on itself until you get the end. Go slowly, use the cloth, and do not tightly roll. Place the strudel on the prepared baking sheet, seam side down, curving it into a horseshoe. Brush again with butter. Bake for 20 minutes, brush one more time with butter, and bake another 15 to 20 minutes or until dough is crispy and deep golden brown. Carefully move to a wire rack and allow to cool 15 minutes before slicing and serving.

Strudel is best eaten the day it is made but can be stored in an airtight container for 1 to 2 days.

FUNKY MONKEY
Drink

The Funky Monkey is a last-day-in-the-dorms special, but it can be tailored for any holiday or event. After any party, wedding, or first communion, if your family is the kind of Catholic who knows how to really let loose, take all the leftover drinks and mix them together, and baby, you got yourself a funky monkey. This concoction can be transformed into a boozy cocktail by adding 1 ounce each of spiced rum, gin, and orange-infused tequila after the ice, but the alcohol-free version is just as wild.

YIELD: 1 drink

4 ounces Founders Day Punch base (page 100)

4 ounces margarita limeade (page 54)

A dash of raspberry rose syrup (page 141)

A squeeze of fresh lemon juice

Fill a highball glass (or solo cup!) with ice. Add, the punch, limeade, raspberry syrup, and squeeze of lemon. Stir and serve.

"Everyone poured all the alcohol they had left into a bowl and that's what's in the cup. Tastes gross, but does the trick."

JANET

HECTOR'S
Tacos

New Haven has at least one thing going for it: Hector's Tacos. Located only ten minutes from Yale, the establishment serves crisp and meaty tacos on warm tortillas. This isn't finger food—this is haute cuisine. Prepare these at home with a garlicky, herby dip and then see if you can beat the record for most tacos eaten at a restaurant that doesn't serve tacos (5).

YIELD: 8 servings

FOR THE CARNITAS

4 to 6 pounds boneless pork shoulder, trimmed and cut into 5-inch strips

2 tablespoons kosher salt

1 to 2 tablespoons oil, for pan

Water

2 teaspoons chili powder

2 teaspoons hot paprika

1 teaspoon ground coriander

1 cinnamon stick

2 dried bay leaves

FOR THE DIP

3 cloves garlic, peeled

4 scallions, white and light green parts only, diced

1 cup fresh cilantro leaves

½ cup fresh parsley leaves

2 tablespoons fresh oregano leaves

3 tablespoons snipped chives

1 teaspoon salt

½ teaspoon cayenne pepper

Juice of 1 lime

1 teaspoon rice vinegar

2 cups (16 ounces) sour cream

Fresh black pepper

TO SERVE

16 corn tortillas

1 white onion, diced

½ cup chopped cilantro leaves

½ cup oil for frying tortillas

Preheat the oven to 350°F. Rub the pork strips with salt and set aside.

To make the carnitas, heat a stovetop-friendly roasting pan on medium-high (you may need to straddle two burners). Coat the pan with oil, and add pork strips, working in small batches if necessary. Brown strips on all sides. Each piece of pork should have a deep golden-brown crust. When all the pork is brown, remove from pan, and set aside.

Add 1 cup of water, chili powder, paprika, coriander, cinnamon stick, and bay leaves to the pan, using the liquid to deglaze the pan of all the crispy brown bits. Return the pork to the pan and add enough water until the pork is about two-thirds submerged.

Braise in the oven for 2½ hours. Check to see whether the meat is pull-apart tender. If not, put it back in the oven for as long as another hour, checking regularly to assess the tenderness. When the pork is completely tender, remove the pan from the oven and shred all of it. Return meat to the oven and roast for another 30 minutes to an hour, until it is deeply caramelized.

TIP: This recipe cooks way down, so don't get stingy on the meat. No one likes a half-filled taco.

To make the dip, in the bowl of a food processor, pulse the garlic until well minced. Add the scallions, cilantro, parsley, oregano, and chives and continue to pulse, scraping down the sides of the bowl, until a pesto-like consistency is reached.

Add the salt, cayenne, lime juice, and vinegar, and pulse to combine. Add sour cream and blend until just smooth. Add pepper to taste. Refrigerate for at least 1 hour to let the flavors meld.

To assemble the tacos, in a large skillet, heat the oil over medium-high. Fry each tortilla for 1 to 2 minutes per side or until they start to bubble. Remove to a cookie sheet lined with paper towel.

Fill each taco with meat, drizzle with the sauce, and add a sprinkle of onion and cilantro.

SPRING BREAK
Fruit Plate

Not everyone is cut out for Spring Break, but Rory and Paris did their best: hangovers, flirting, cute boys, and lots of bad food. The Spring Break Fruit Plate was a fresh respite after they ate vending machine food for a week (because, remember, those bananas from the banana eating contest are not actually for eating). You can tweak this with your own favorite Floridian fruit combo to dunk in the tropical coconut dip. Don't forget to tip your waiter.

YIELD: 6 to 8 servings

FOR THE DIP
⅔ cup shredded, unsweetened coconut

1 cup nonfat Greek vanilla yogurt

1 cup sour cream

2 tablespoons brown sugar, packed

Juice of one lime

FOR THE FRUIT PLATE
1 pound strawberries, rinsed and hulled

1 small pineapple, skinned, cored, and cut into 2- to 3-inch pieces

1 small watermelon, cut into 2- to 3-inch pieces

2 mangos, skinned and cut into wedges

To make the dip, over medium-high heat, heat a small, dry skillet for 2 to 3 minutes. Add the coconut, and, stirring constantly, toast for 1 to 2 minutes. Remove from heat and stir occasionally until just starting to brown and become fragrant, 2 to 3 minutes. Transfer to a plate and allow to cool completely, about 15 minutes.

In a small serving bowl, combine the yogurt, sour cream, brown sugar, and lime juice. Stir until thoroughly combined. Gently fold in the toasted coconut. Cover and refrigerate until ready to serve.

On a large serving platter, arrange all the fruit pieces around the bowl of dip and serve.

"Now we're going to need a fruit plate in about an hour and keep the iced tea coming."

PARIS

CHRISTMAS
Apple Tarts

The Christmas party at the Gilmore mansion is the one Richard-and-Emily event each year that Lorelai actually looks forward to, so she's crushed when Emily uninvites her one year. No Christmas party means no Christmas apple tarts, a sweet treat Lorelai spends the entire year waiting for, dreaming about, and composing love songs for. These tarts are spiced with cinnamon and cloves and drizzled with caramel. Here's the recipe so you never have to suffer a Christmas without them.

YIELD: 12 to 14 tarts

8 tablespoons butter, plus more for greasing

4 crisp apples, quartered, cored, and sliced thin

4 teaspoons lemon juice

1 teaspoon cinnamon

½ teaspoon cloves

1 cup sugar

1 pastry recipe form Perfect Peach Pie (page 35)

Grease a 12-cup muffin tin thoroughly with butter. Roll out the pastry dough to about ⅛-inch thick. Cut out 3½-inch circles and press gently into the bottom of each muffin tin cavity. Keep the sides as straight as possible and make sure the dough goes all the way to the bottom of the tin. Flatten small pleats as necessary. Reserve the dough scraps to create leaves, if desired. Chill in the refrigerator while you prepare the apples.

Toss the sliced apples in the lemon juice, cinnamon, and cloves. In a large skillet over medium heat, melt the butter and then sprinkle the sugar over it. Place the apples in a single layer only overlapping slightly when necessary. Turn heat to medium-high and cook until the syrup turns to a dark amber, 7 to 10 minutes, flipping the apples halfway through with a fork. Decant to a heatproof bowl and set aside.

Preheat the oven to 425°F.

Place apple slices along the sides of each tart shell, overlapping slightly. Continue with more slices, working toward the center to create a rose shape. Finish by rolling a slice of apple to create the center. Repeat until all the tart shells are filled. Reserve extra caramel for drizzling.

Bake for 20 to 25 minutes or until the crusts are golden brown.

Allow to cool for 5 minutes. Press down any apples that may have popped up during baking. Use a small offset spatula to gently remove the tarts from the tin and transfer to a wire rack. Drizzle with additional caramel. Serve warm or at room temperature.

Tarts can be stored in an airtight container for up to 2 days. For decoration, roll out the remaining pastry dough and use leaf cookie cutters to cut out. Chill for 10 minutes, sprinkle with cinnamon sugar, and bake at 350°F for 5 to 8 minutes or until golden brown.

LORELAI: *"I can live without the apple tarts."*

RORY: *"You've made up songs after eating five of them with lyrics that contradict that last statement."*

CONCLUSION: *Bon Voyage*

Some people come into Stars Hollow and stay only for a short while—Christopher, Jess Mariano, Christiane Amanpour—but some people will always belong there. Even though we last see Rory leaving Stars Hollow to hit the campaign trail, everyone knew she'd be back. After all, a person can only go so long without Luke's donuts, Sookie's marvelous main courses, and Lorelai's cozy albeit culinary-deficient kitchen.

From weird dates with Kirk to Friday Night Dinners, sharing a meal is always a foolproof way to ensure a moment of togetherness. Every potluck and picnic basket auction is a reason for the community to convene and lend their support or air their grievances. So, when you want to get the gang together, lure them over with a batch of dessert sushi, a savory lobster pot pie, or a rich chocolate cake. They won't be able to say no—if temptation leads, they will follow.

"Um. I hope you're good. I want you to be good, and, um, okay, so, goodbye. That word sounds really lame and stupid right now, but there it is. Goodbye."

RORY

ABOUT *the* AUTHORS

ELENA PONS CRAIG is a food and prop stylist, recipe developer, and cookbook contributor with more than 25 years of experience in the world of culinary design, marketing, photography, and publication. She has a deep love for pop culture, super-fans, and hiding Easter eggs. With the help of her husband and their two children, she has developed superhero cooking skills that cross generations, genders, and genres. Visit epcfoodstyling.com for more of her food and prop styling.

KRISTEN MULROONEY is a writer, editor, and stress-baker. Her writing can be found in The New Yorker and McSweeney's, and she has contributed to and worked as an editor for The Belladonna. Her words and wisdom on the pitfalls of parenting appear in McSweeney's humor anthology *Embrace the Merciless Joy*. Kristen lives in Massachusetts with her husband, dog, and three kids who were delighted to eat all the desserts she stress-baked while writing this book. Visit kristenmulrooney.com for more of her humor and writing.

ACKNOWLEDGEMENTS

ELENA PONS CRAIG – I would like to dedicate this book to my children, both of whom have always brought an incredible sense of humor to my life and consisitently remind me of the importance of having fun. I also want to thank Insight Editions, Zero Cool Studios, and my editor, Anna Wostenberg.

KRISTEN MULROONEY – A big thank you to Anna Wostenberg and Elena Craig—I couldn't have dreamed of a better team to work with on this wonderful project! Thank you to Joanne Ogrean and Krysta Stuart for sharing their insight and encyclopedic knowledge. And all of my love and gratitude to Matthew, Adam, Matilda, and Greta for their patience and support during my binge-watch (I was working!) and always.

"I stop drinking coffee. I stop doing the standing and the walking and the words-putting-into-sentence doing."

LORELAI

DIETARY *Considerations*

V = Vegetarian   V+ = Vegan
GF = Gluten-free   V*, V+* & GF* = Easily made vegetarian, vegan, or gluten-free with simple alterations

LUKE'S DINER

	GF	V	V+
Coffee in an IV	GF	V	V+
Hot Fudge Sundae With Grapefruit on the Side	GF	V	
Fluffy Buttermilk Pancakes		V	
Caesar's Salad	GF		V+
Delicious Donuts		V	
Chicken Noodle Soup	GF*		
Side of Mashed Potatoes	GF	V	
Danish Day Danishes		V	
Perfect Peach Pie		V	
Caesar's Chilaquiles!	GF*	V	V+*

THE INDEPENDENCE INN, THE DRAGONFLY INN, & SOOKIE ST. JAMES'S CREATIONS

	GF	V	V+
Roquefort Puffs		V	
Jackson's Blueberry Shortcake		V	
Sookie's Magic Risotto	GF		
Sookie's Wedding Cupcakes		V	
Deep-Fried Turkey Leg	GF		
Medieval Feast Plum Pudding		V	
Sookie's Critically Acclaimed Zucchini Soup	GF	V	V+
Jalapeño-Chipotle Mac & Cheese		V	
Lorelai's Graduation Cake		V	
Broccoli Tarts		V	
Ciabatta Bun Caprese Sandwiches		V	
Sookie's Roasted Acorn Squash Soup	GF	V	V+*
Norman Mailer's Legendary Iced Tea	GF	V	V+
Handkerchief Pasta With Brown Butter Sauce		V	

A STARS HOLLOW POTLUCK

	GF	V	V+
Mrs. Kim's Eggless Egg Salad Sandwiches	GF*	V	V+
Mrs. Kim's Everything-Free Muffin Drops & Tea	GF	V	V+
Lane's Wedding Dumplings		V	V+
Pasta 3 Ways for Rory & Dean's Three-Month Anniversary:			
Fettucini Alfredo		V	
Cashew Chicken	GF		
Vegetable Chow Mein		V	
Red Velvet Cake		V	
Lorelai's Giant Birthday Pizza		V*	
Ye Olde Butter Brickle Crunch Ice Cream	GF	V	
Steak & Six Baked Potatoes for Four People	GF		
Potatoes		V	
Shrimp From Al's Pancake World	GF		
Founder's Day Punch	GF	V	V+

LORELAI & RORY'S HOUSE

	GF	V	V+
Homemade Edible Cookie Dough	GF	V	
Rory's Pretzels From Around the World		V	
Lime Fantasy Supreme With Two Spoons	GF	V	
Dessert Sushi		V	
Cream Puffs for Hands		V	
Frozen Pizza With Tater Tots		V*	
Complete Salad in a Bag			V+
Homemade Peanut Butter Sandwich Cookies		V	
Nachos & a Slushie	GF*	V*	
Gin Martini No Onion	GF	V	V+
Apple & Cherry Turnovers		V	
Homemade Toaster Pastries		V	

BEYOND STARS HOLLOW

	GF	V	V+
Pot Roast, Potatoes, & Rolls:			
Pot Roast	GF		
Potatoes	GF	V	
Rolls		V	
Chocolate Cake & Coffee		V	
Emily's Tailgate Bloody Marys	GF		
Mashed Banana on Toast	GF*	V	V+
The Rory Drink	GF	V	
Funky Monkey Drink	GF	V	V+
Spring Break Fruit Plate	GF	V	
Rosa's Strudel		V	
Christmas Apple Tarts		V	

GLOSSARY

Blanch and Shock: Blanching is the process of bringing water to a boil, adding food, most commonly vegetables or fruits, to the water and cooking for a quick time, normally 1 to 3 minutes. To stop the cooking process from going too far, the food is removed from the boiling water and plunged into an ice bath (½ water and ½ ice) to cool before it is drained and used in the recipe.

Blooming Gelatin: Blooming gelatin helps ensure the gelatin will dissolve easily and create a smooth finished product. Using the amount of water and gelatin asked for in the recipe, place the water in a shallow bowl and sprinkle the gelatin evenly over the surface. Allow the gelatin to bloom for 3 to 5 minutes. Visually, you will see the changes as the gelatin begins to absorb the water and swell.

Butter: Butter, unless otherwise noted, is salted butter.

Chiffonade: This French term means "little ribbons." It is the method of taking leaves, such as basil, and stacking them together, rolling them up, and then thinly slicing them to create thin ribbons of garnish.

Deglaze: Deglazing is adding liquid, usually wine or stock, to a hot pan to release all of the caramelized food from the pan. These caramelized bits, called fond, are full of flavor and should not be left behind. Deglazing is often the first step in making a delicious sauce.

Egg Wash: Whisk together 1 egg and 1 tablespoon of water until light and foamy. Use a pastry brush to apply when the recipe requires.

Fry Station and Safety: If you're making something that requires deep frying, here are some important tips to prevent you from setting your house (and yourself) on fire:

- If you don't have a dedicated deep fryer, use a Dutch oven or a high-walled sauté pan.
- Never have too much oil in the pan! You don't want hot oil spilling out as soon as you put the food in.
- Only use a suitable cooking oil, like canola, peanut, or vegetable oil.
- Always keep track of the oil temperature with a thermometer. 350°F to 375°F should do the trick.
- Never put too much food in the pan at the same time!
- Never put wet food in the pan. It will splatter and may cause burns.
- Always have a lid nearby to cover the pan in case it starts to spill over or catch fire. A properly rated fire extinguisher is also great to have on hand in case of emergencies.
- Never leave the pan unattended and never let children near the pan.
- Never, ever put your face, hand, or any other body part in the hot oil.

Macerate: Fruit mixed with sugar and/or some citrus juice is set aside to soften and release its natural juices. This is known as macerating.

Milk: The word milk in this book is always referring to dairy milk unless otherwise noted. In most cases any percentage of milk fat will do unless otherwise noted.

Salt: Feel free to use your salt of choice unless it has been noted in the recipe. Kosher salt is the one most commonly used throughout the book.

Silicone Baking Mat: Silicone baking mats can be used up to high temperatures in the oven and used in the freezer. They are very helpful in baking because they are easy to roll dough out on and can then go from prep station to chilling to oven without having to move dough. They are extremely non-stick and easy to clean.

Vanilla Paste versus Vanilla Extract: Vanilla bean paste give you the strong vanilla flavor and the beautiful vanilla bean flecks without having to split and steep a vanilla bean. While it is more expensive than extract, there are recipes where it will really shine and elevate a dish. When it will make a wonderful addition to a dish, it has been called out, but it can always be replaced with vanilla extract with a one for one swap out.

MEASUREMENT *Conversions*

VOLUME

US	Metric
⅕ teaspoon (tsp)	1 ml
1 teaspoon (tsp)	5 ml
1 tablespoon (tbsp)	15 ml
1 fluid ounce (fl. oz.)	30 ml
⅕ cup	50 ml
¼ cup	60 ml
⅔ cup	80 ml
3.4 fluid ounces (fl. oz.)	100 ml
½ cup	120 ml
⅔ cup	160 ml
¾ cup	180 ml
1 cup	240 ml
1 pint (2 cups)	480 ml
1 quart (4 cups)	.95 liter

TEMPERATURES

Fahrenheit	Celsius
200°	93.3°
212°	100°
250°	120°
275°	135°
300°	150°
325°	163°
350°	177°
400°	205°
425°	218°
450°	232°
475°	246°

WEIGHT

US	Metric
0.5 ounce (oz.)	14 grams (g)
1 ounce (oz.)	28 grams (g)
¼ pound (lb.)	113 grams (g)
⅓ pound (lb.)	151 grams (g)
½ pound (lb.)	227 grams (g)
1 pound (lb.)	454 grams (g)

NOTES

NOTES

INDEX

A

Apple & Cherry Turnovers, 123

B

Baked Potatoes, 95
Baked Ziti, 82

BEEF

Baked Ziti, 82
Beef Noodle Salad, 97
Classic Luke's Diner Cheeseburger, 20
Classic Pot Roast, 131
Penne With Beef Ragu, 85
Santa Burger, 25
Steak, 94

BEVERAGES

coffee, brewing tips, 15
Emily's Tailgate Bloody Marys, 142
Founder's Day Punch, 100
Funky Monkey Drink, 154
Gin Martini No Onion, 139
Nachos & a Slushie, 122
Norman Mailer's Legendary Iced Tea, 67
The Rory Drink, 141
Sookie's Survival Margaritas, 54

Blueberry Shortcake, 42

BREADS

Everything Parker House Rolls, 131–132
Mashed Bananas on Toast, 144

BREAKFAST

Apple & Cherry Turnovers, 123
Caesar's Chilaquiles!, 36
Danish Day Danishes, 33
Delicious Donuts, 28–29
Fluffy Buttermilk Pancakes, 19
Homemade Toaster Pastries, 125

Luke's Special Omelet, 17
Mrs. Kim's Everything-Free
    Muffin Drops & Tea, 76
Rosa's Strudel, 153

Brewing coffee, 15
Butter Brickle Crunch Ice Cream, 91

C

Caesar's Chilaquiles!, 36
Caesar's Salad, 27

CAKES

Chocolate Cake & Coffee, 134–135
Lorelai's Graduation Cake, 59–60
Red Velvet Cake, 90
Sookie's Wedding Cake &
    Cupcakes, 47–48

Cashew Chicken, 86
Cheeseburger, 20

CHICKEN

Cashew Chicken, 86
Chicken Noodle Soup, 30
Chili Cheese Fries, 26
Chocolate Cake & Coffee, 134–135
Christmas Apple Tarts, 159
Ciabatta Bun Caprese Sandwiches, 63
Classic Luke's Diner Cheeseburger, 20
Classic Pot Roast, 131

COCKTAILS

Emily's Tailgate Bloody Marys, 142
Funky Monkey Drink, 154
Gin Martini No Onion, 139
The Rory Drink, 141
Sookie's Survival Margaritas, 54

Coffee, brewing tips, 15
Complete Salad in a Bag, 119
Cookie dough, 109

COOKIES

Homemade Edible Cookie Dough, 106
Homemade Peanut Butter Sandwich
    Cookies, 116

Cream Puffs for Hands, 114

D

Danish Day Danishes, 33
Dark Chocolate Pudding, 138
Deep-Fried Turkey Leg, 50
Delicious Donuts, 28–29
Dessert Sushi, 115

DESSERTS

Apple & Cherry Turnovers, 123
Chocolate Cake & Coffee, 134–135
Christmas Apple Tarts, 159
Cream Puffs for Hands, 116
Danish Day Danishes, 33
Dark Chocolate Pudding, 138
Delicious Donuts, 28–29
Dessert Sushi, 115
Homemade Edible Cookie Dough, 109
Homemade Peanut Butter Sandwich
    Cookies, 106
Homemade Toaster Pastries, 125
Hot Fudge Sundae With Grapefruit on
    the Side, 16
Jackson's Blueberry Shortcake, 42
Lime Fantasy Supreme With
    Two Spoons, 112
Lorelai's Graduation Cake, 59–60
Medieval Feast Plum Pudding, 51
Mrs. Kim's Everything-Free
    Muffin Drops & Tea, 76
Mrs. Kim's Extra Chunky Multigrain
    Pudding, 77
Perfect Peach Pie, 35
Red Velvet Cake, 90

Rosa's Strudel, 153

Sookie's Wedding Cake &
    Cupcakes, 47–48

Ye Olde Butter Brickle Crunch
    Ice Cream, 91

Donuts, 28–29

Dumplings, 78–81

E

EGGS

Caesar's Chilaquiles!, 36

Luke's Special Omelet, 17

Mrs. Kim's Eggless Egg Salad
    Sandwiches, 75

Emily's Tailgate Bloody Marys, 142

Everything Parker House Rolls, 131–132

F

Fettuccini Alfredo, 83

Fluffy Buttermilk Pancakes, 19

Founder's Day Punch, 100

Frozen foods, baking, 126

Frozen Pizza With Tater Tots, 118

FRUIT

Apple & Cherry Turnovers, 123

Christmas Apple Tarts, 159

Homemade Toaster Pastries, 125

Hot Fudge Sundae With Grapefruit on
    the Side, 16

Jackson's Blueberry Shortcake, 42

Mashed Bananas on Toast, 144

Medieval Feast Plum Pudding, 51

Perfect Peach Pie, 35

Spring Break Fruit Plate, 157

Funky Monkey Drink, 154

G

Gazpacho, 145

Gin Martini No Onion, 139

H

Handkerchief Pasta With Brown Butter
    Sauce, 70-71

Hector's Tacos, 156

Homemade Edible Cookie Dough, 109

Homemade Peanut Butter Sandwich
    Cookies, 106

Homemade Toaster Pastries, 125

Hot Fudge Sundae With Grapefruit
    on the Side, 16

I

ICE CREAM

Hot Fudge Sundae With Grapefruit
    on the Side, 16

Ye Olde Butter Brickle Crunch
    Ice Cream, 91

Iced tea, 67

J

Jackson's Blueberry Shortcake, 42

Jalapeño-Chipotle Mac & Cheese, 56

Johnny Machette's Pasta Casserole, 149

L

Lamb sandwich, 152

Lane's Wedding Dumplings, 78–81

Leftovers, reheating, 126

Lime Fantasy Supreme with
    Two Spoons, 112

Lobster Bisque, 57

Lobster Pot Pie, 146

Lorelai's Giant Birthday Pizza, 92

Lorelai's Graduation Cake, 59–60

Luke's Health-Conscious Turkey
    Burger, 23

Luke's Special Omelet, 17

M

Mac & cheese, 56

MAIN DISHES.
SEE ALSO BREAKFAST; SANDWICHES

Baked Ziti, 82

Cashew Chicken, 86

Classic Pot Roast, 131

Deep-Fried Turkey Leg, 50

Fettuccini Alfredo, 83

Frozen Pizza With Tater Tots, 118

Handkerchief Pasta With Brown Butter
    Sauce, 70-71

Hector's Tacos, 156

Jalapeño-Chipotle Mac & Cheese, 56

Johnny Machette's Pasta Casserole, 149

Lobster Pot Pie, 146

Lorelai's Giant Birthday Pizza, 92

Penne With Beef Ragu, 85

Shrimp From Al's Pancake World, 98

Sookie's Magic Risotto, 44

Steak, 94

Vegetable Chow Mein, 89

Margaritas, 54

Mashed Bananas on Toast, 144

Mashed Potatoes, 31

Medieval Feast Plum Pudding, 51

Movie Night Snack Board, 105

Mrs. Kim's Eggless Egg Salad
    Sandwiches, 75

Mrs. Kim's Everything-Free
    Muffin Drops & Tea, 76

Mrs. Kim's Extra Chunky Multigrain
    Pudding, 77

Muffin Drops, 76

N

Nachos & a Slushie, 122

Norman Mailer's Legendary Iced Tea, 67

Nuts, spiced, 148

O

Ordering takeout, 126

P

Pancakes, 19

PASTA

Baked Ziti, 82

Fettuccini Alfredo, 83

Handkerchief Pasta With Brown Butter Sauce, 70-71

Johnny Machette's Pasta Casserole, 149

Penne With Beef Ragu, 85

Peanut butter sandwich cookies, 106

Penne with Beef Ragu, 85

Perfect Peach Pie, 35

PIES

Lobster Pot Pie, 146

Perfect Peach Pie, 35

PIZZA

Frozen Pizza With Tater Tots, 118

Lorelai's Giant Birthday Pizza, 92

Plum pudding, 51

Pork tacos, 156

Pot roast, 131

POTATOES

Baked Potatoes, 95

Chili Cheese Fries, 26

Classic Pot Roast, 131

Frozen Pizza With Tater Tots, 118

Mashed Potatoes, 31

Pretzels, 110-111

PUDDING

chocolate, 138

plum, 51

soy, 77

R

Red Velvet Cake, 90

Reheating leftovers, 126

Risotto, 44

Roasted Acorn Squash Soup, 64

Roquefort Puffs, 41

The Rory Drink, 141

Rory's Pretzels From Around the World, 110-111

Rosa's Lamb Sandwich, 152

Rosa's Strudel, 153

S

SALADS

Beef Noodle Salad, 97

Caesar's Salad, 27

Complete Salad in a Bag, 119

Salmon Puffs, 151

SANDWICHES

Ciabatta Bun Caprese Sandwiches, 63

Classic Luke's Diner Cheeseburger, 20

Luke's Health-Conscious Turkey Burger, 23

Mrs. Kim's Eggless Egg Salad Sandwiches, 75

Rosa's Lamb Sandwich, 152

Santa Burger, 25

SEAFOOD

Lobster Bisque, 57

Lobster Pot Pie, 146

Salmon Puffs, 151

Shrimp From Al's Pancake World, 98

Sookie's Magic Risotto, 44

SIDE DISHES

Baked Potatoes, 95

Chili Cheese Fries, 26

Jalapeño-Chipotle Mac & Cheese, 56

Mashed Potatoes, 31

SNACKS

Movie Night Snack Board, 105

Nachos & a Slushie, 122

Roquefort Puffs, 41

Rory's Pretzels From Around the World, 110-111

Salmon Puffs, 151

Spring Break Fruit Plate, 157

Trix's Spiced Nuts, 148

Wallowing Board, 121

Sookie's Critically Acclaimed Zucchini Soup, 53

Sookie's Magic Risotto, 44

Sookie's Survival Margaritas, 54

Sookie's Wedding Cake & Cupcakes, 47–48

SOUPS

Chicken Noodle Soup, 30

Gazpacho, 145

Lobster Bisque, 57

Roasted Acorn Squash Soup, 64

Sookie's Critically Acclaimed Zucchini Soup, 53

Soy pudding, 77

Spiced nuts, 148

Spring Break Fruit Plate, 157

Steak, 94

Strudel, 153

T

Tacos, 156

Takeout, ordering/reheating, 126

Tarts, 159

Toaster pastries, 125

Trix's Spiced Nuts, 148

TURKEY

Deep-Fried Turkey Leg, 50

Luke's Health-Conscious Turkey
    Burger, 23

Turnovers, 123

V

Vegetable Chow Mein, 89

VEGETABLES. SEE ALSO SALADS

Gazpacho, 145

Roasted Acorn Squash Soup, 64

Sookie's Critically Acclaimed
    Zucchini Soup, 53

Vegetable Chow Mein, 89

W

Wallowing Board, 121

Y

Ye Olde Butter Brickle Crunch
    Ice Cream, 91

Z

Zucchini soup, 53

TITAN
BOOKS

144 Southwark Street
London SE1 0UP
www.titanbooks.com

 Find us on Facebook: www.facebook.com/titanbooks

 Follow us on X: @titanbooks

A CIP catalogue record for this title is available from the British
Library.

ISBN: 978-1-80336-060-7

Publisher: Raoul Goff
VP of Licensing and Partnerships: Vanessa Lopez
VP of Creative: Chrissy Kwasnik
VP of Manufacturing: Alix Nicholaeff
Editorial Director: Vicki Jaeger
Senior Designer: Judy Wiatrek Trum
Editor: Anna Wostenberg
Associate Editor: Maya Alpert
Editorial Assistant: Grace Orriss
Production Editor: Jan Neal
Production Manager: Sam Taylor
Sr. Prod-Mgr Subsidiary Rights: Lina s Palma-Temena

Photographer: Ted Thomas
Food & Prop Stylist: Elena P. Craig
Assistant Food Sylist: August Craig

ROOTS of PEACE   REPLANTED PAPER

Insight Editions, in association with Roots of Peace, will plant two trees for each
tree used in the manufacturing of this book. Roots of Peace is an internationally
renowned humanitarian organization dedicated to eradicating land mines
worldwide and converting war-torn lands into productive farms and wildlife habitats.
Roots of Peace will plant two million fruit and nut trees in Afghanistan and provide
farmers there with the skills and support necessary for sustainable land use.

Manufactured in China by Insight Editions

10 9 8 7 6 5